Citizen Power

A Mandate for Change

Senator Mike Gravel

Foreword by Ralph Nader

authorHOUSE®

AuthorHouse™
1663 Liberty Drive, Suite 200
Bloomington, IN 47403
www.authorhouse.com
Phone: 1-800-839-8640

First published by AuthorHouse   2/6/2008

ISBN: 978-1-4343-4315-4 (sc)

Library of Congress Control Number: 2008900708

Printed in the United States of America
Bloomington, Indiana

This book is printed on acid-free paper.

Cover design by Jeff Rosenplot

To Whitney,
The love of my life

And to my grandchildren
Renee, Alex, Madison & Mackenzie

And their parents
Martin & LizaBeth
Lynne & Drake

With love and hope for the future

Acknowledgments

Books seldom are written without a great deal of assistance and encouragement from friends and associates. This book is no exception.

With respect to the original *Citizen Power*, my thanks to the wonderful women on my staff, whose abilities and efficiency made it possible for me to find the time to write a book without diminishing the effectiveness of my office: Flora Bergman, Dianne Church, Susan Gordon, Roselynn Heath, Marcia Miller, Elisabeth Romayko, Betsy Schoenfeld, Alice Slater, Jill Smythe, and Kathy Morgan.

My gratitude to those who contributed many of the thoughts and writings from which much of the finished product was drawn: Dr. Len Rodberg, Dr. Douglas Jones, Dr. Tom Lantos, Bill Hoffman, Egan O'Connor, Arlie Schardt, Joe Rothstein, Karl Hess, Marcus Raskin, Charles Fishman, Tom Smythe, Ted Johnson, Tom Reeves, and Michael Rowan. Also, my appreciation to many others too numerous to list here for their helpful suggestions and thoughtful comments.

Special acknowledgment and deep personal gratitude to the two men who served as my chief editorial consultants and advisers throughout the compilation and the preparation of this work in 1971: Bill Howard and my administrative assistant, Marty Wolf, and his patient wife, Sonia.

Since the original text in 1971, my efforts have centered on the development of the National Initiative. My work would not have been possible without the creative participation of Donald Kemner, David Parish, Charles Turk, Sylvia Shih, John Sutter, Esther Franklin, and in honor of the work of Ed and Joyce Koupal.

For this current edition, I express sincere gratitude to Susan Giffin, Stacy Standley, David Eisenbach, Laurence J. Kotlikoff, Victor Fuchs, Joe Lauria, Mike Gray, Ralph Nader, and to Vid Beldavs of AuthorHouse.

With special appreciation to my 2008 campaign staff, advisers, and support team: Chris Petherick, Elliott Jacobson, Alex Colvin, April Shapley, Jose Rodriguez, Eli Israel, Jim Brauner, Augustine Gyamfi, Michael Grant, Skyler McKinley, Lynne Mosier, Dick Thomas, Deborah Petri, Alexander Rosenberg, David Nelson-VanDette, Beckey Isaiah, Mindi Iden, Jim Dupont, Jon Kraus, Marie and Tom Lombardi, Tom Lombardi Jr., George Ripley, Michael Szymanski, Mike Foudy, Richard Rebh, Peter Peckarsky, Paul Linet, Rob Ryan, Hans Barbe, Dan Connor, Jeff Rammelt, David and Hi-Jin Hodge, George Rebh, Josh LeKoch, Wayne Madsen, James McCrink, Jeffrey & Cici Peters, Greg Piccionelli, Larry Rothenberg, Catherine Hand, Jim Stork, Ron Ansin, Lynn Stewart, David Weisman, Theresa Wrangham, Afifa Klouj, Phil Davis, Casey McIlvaine, Jake Futerfas, and two of the most unusual supporters of my political career, Greg Chase and Jeff Tausch.

Foreword

Like a fresh wind coming from Alaska, the state he represented as a U.S. Senator from 1969 to 1981, Mike Gravel is determined to start a debate about the fundamentals of democracy.

Throughout his work in public service, Senator Gravel has understood that politics is about power—who has it, who should have it, who misuses it, and how it can be used to the betterment of human life here and around the world. He not only understands it, as the cliché has it, he also has walked the walk.

As a senator, he became known for releasing the controversial *Pentagon Papers* at an *ad hoc* committee performance. He was early against the Vietnam War. He was early in advocating diplomatic relations with China. More recently, Senator Gravel was opposed to the War in Iraq even before this quagmire and criminal endeavor began. He opposes military action against a completely United States-surrounded Iran. He understands the inequities in the Israeli occupation of Palestine.

Senator Gravel knows that elections have been commercialized to the point where the very media expectation of candidates is determined by how much money they've raised in every quarter. It's almost like a corporation: What is the quarterly report? Money from commercial interests, such as the drug industry, the oil industry, the nuclear industry, the auto industry, the banking industry, and insurance industries, with their 10,000 political action committees, comes heavily in terms of *quid pro quos*. They are rarely specific about what they want in return.

Senator Gravel understands what very few candidates are willing to understand and demonstrate publicly. Now more than ever, this country needs a shift in power from the few to the many. He understands that we must make the domination of just about everything by giant corporations a major issue. These giant corporations see no boundaries to their hegemony, to their greed, to their abandonment of our country, to the control of communities, to the infiltration of elections, and to the control of every department and agency in the U.S. government, including the Department of Labor. With their political appointments, their thousands of political action committees, and with their 35,000 lobbyists—if you don't make this a major issue, it will affect our economy and our electoral reforms, and we will be avoiding a critical issue and engaging in rhetorical charades, slogans, clichés, and self-censorship.

If money is the index of electoral politics, Senator Gravel rightly believes our democracy is gone. We're supposed to have a government of the people, by the people, and for the people. There can be no democracy if it is a government of the Exxons, by the General Motors, for the DuPonts.

For over a decade, given the failures of elected politicians, Senator Gravel has been engaged in some extraordinary research and consultations with leading constitutional law experts about the need to enact another check to the faltering checks and balances—namely, the National Initiative for Democracy—a proposed law that empowers the people as lawmakers.

In recognizing this, Senator Gravel has convened conferences of some of the finest constitutional law experts in the country. He has engaged them in a fundamental debate regarding the plenary power of the American people to enact their own laws, rooted in the Declaration of Independence, a juridical document, not just a protest, the U.S. Constitution, the Federalist Papers.

Senator Gravel's National Initiative for Democracy is the most fundamental proposal I have ever seen or read about by any candidate in any major party in the United States. It is not a proposal that can be reduced to "sound bites" on television. It cannot be compressed in seven seconds and 42 nanoseconds. It has to challenge our willingness to engage in a deliberative electoral process where people are given a chance to interact with the candidates, to propose their own agendas, and to meet with them all over the country as they campaign. There will be no more manipulation of the voters into spectators, and there will be no more simply viewing the electoral process as entertainment funded by commercial interests and beyond the range of effective political action on the part of the voters.

What Senator Gravel is conveying to the country is a wisdom embodied in the definition of freedom by Marcus Cicero over 2,000 years ago in ancient Rome. That prominent orator and lawyer defined freedom in a way that forces us to confront its denial or its substance— not its rhetorical flourish by manipulative politicians indentured to commercial and corporate interest. According to Cicero, that definition is the following: "Freedom is participation in power." This is the key element that is launching Senator Gravel into one state after another with his proposals. And that could be the mantra for Mike Gravel's 2008 presidential campaign.

Ralph Nader

Contents

Introduction

When I decided to run for president, I decided to re-issue *Citizen Power*. My initial hope was that it would be a second edition. Upon rereading it, however, two things stood out: 1) the total disappointment upon realizing that the problems I defined 37 years ago had grown considerably worse; and 2) my hopes of having to do very little rewriting were dashed by the fact that some of my views had matured and changed, requiring new and different solutions to the problems I thought I had figured out.

The entire economic section has been left out, because I cannot begin to do justice in the amount of time I have available; nevertheless I have some unusual programs that I hope to undertake when I become president.

I added a chapter on the drug war which, of course, started with Richard Nixon just about the time I was writing *Citizen Power*. The War on Drugs occasioned the whole debacle of prison expansion, and I felt compelled to address both of these serious problems which seem to scare other progressive candidates.

In the chapter on taxation that I wrote 37 years ago, I recognized the corruption of the income tax and advocated a single tax. However, the work that has been done on the Fair Tax was superior to what I had done more than three decades earlier. I therefore found it easy to support the Fair Tax with its progressive rebate. Of course, with our present fiscal gap, the Fair Tax now becomes the only possible solution.

My healthcare proposal probably represents the most substantial change. At the time, I naively assumed that a total government program could meet our requirements. As a result of my personal experiences with government programs and the innate abuse of government power, I departed from what I would call not a single-payer but a single-source solution. That's why I amalgamated a program from two sources that meld together the checks and balances involving all the stakeholders in the healthcare field.

The warfare state that I defined as a result of the Vietnam War has been expanded to include the Iraq War, but mostly to address the military-industrial complex, the existence of which mandates the repetition of wars periodically; otherwise, there are no profits to be made by the industrial part of the partnership and no promotions within the military arm.

Probably the most discouraging chapter is the one on secrecy. Thirty-six years ago, I had just released the *Pentagon Papers* and my case was before the Supreme Court; I was unsure of the outcome. Nevertheless, I was optimistic, which characterizes my whole approach in the original *Citizen Power*. Bear in mind, I was at the beginning of my Senate career and had great confidence that changes could be brought about within representative government. It was only at the end of my career when I left office that I was totally discouraged over the inability of representative government to address the problems that face us all. The secrecy issue was terrible under Richard Nixon, and it has only become worse in succeeding Democratic and Republican administrations.

The chapter on global governance articulates a view I have had since I was in my teens when I read *The Anatomy of Peace* by Emory Reeve. In it, he stated that until there is some form of global governance, mankind will never enjoy peace or a fair distribution of the planet's resources. As a result of my experiences and studies on global governance, I have now written a specific plan that defines the kind of global governance that would work fairly for everyone. It is a restructured United Nations that would require little change in the U.N. Charter, which is a magnificent document. What will facilitate this change is essentially the subject of Chapter 2, which I view as the most important contribution of this book and, I hope, the most important contribution of my life as a public servant.

The creation of a legislative proposal—the National Initiative for Democracy—is nothing less than an effort to bring about a fundamental change in the paradigm of human governance. Certainly, it is not the most modest undertaking, but in essence a very simple one; and that is that human beings with rational will are more than capable to govern themselves. They merely need a structure to do it in a common-sense fashion.

I apologize for the many shortcomings that you will find in this book. I do not consider myself a scholar, but I do consider myself very much of a knowledge junkie, and I respect wisdom, which I do not think is based on education alone but on life's experiences.

My writing is self-taught. The acquisition of knowledge, for me, is a thrilling experience that I have sought all my life and have chosen to share through a career of public service and now through a modest literary effort.

I hope that this book strikes a chord of interest and becomes a catalyst for thought and discussion.

Mike Gravel
December 7, 2007

1

Now It's the Citizen's Turn

There can be no democracy unless it is
a dynamic democracy.
When our people cease to participate—to have
a place in the sun— then all of us will
wither in the darkness of decadence.
Saul D. Alinsky

"BULLSHIT, Senator. It won't work."

"Why not?"

"Because you're talking about something that doesn't exist, man, that's why. There's no such thing as citizen power. Not for people like us."

The black youth tilted his chair back against the wall and regarded me with open skepticism, challenging me to prove him wrong. The others nodded their agreement.

It was a hot summer afternoon in mid-1970, and I was in a Harlem storefront street academy, talking with a group of social and educational drop-outs—the ones polite society paternalistically refers to as "the disadvantaged." I had scheduled the visit when I arrived in New York earlier in the day and learned I had some free time before my evening speaking engagement. The street academy program was getting some good reviews. I wanted to see one for myself, and I wanted to talk with the students.

For months, I had sensed a "happening" taking place in America. Everywhere I traveled, I saw growing public dissatisfaction, frustration and anger. That was no silent majority I was witnessing. They were people articulating in both words and deeds that they wanted something more out of life than they were receiving. They were demanding more economic security, more benefits and safeguards, more personal freedom, and more control over the decision-making process.

The demands were not particularly new, but there was something significantly different about the manner in which they were being presented. Instead of complaining and demonstrating individually, citizens were joining together and forming powerful public-interest constituencies: blacks, Latinos, peace groups, the young, the aged, women, homosexuals, environmentalists, welfare mothers, consumers—each with their own specific objectives and proposals, yet all sharing the common bond of seeking to change the status quo in America, to improve it, and to have some impact on society.

Out of the seeds of despair, conflict, and alienation, I detected, and probably others also did, that the embryo of new citizen empowerment was taking shape—a program for change—struggling to achieve life. A new force was emerging upon the American scene: citizen power. All that was needed, I felt, was public awareness of that power and the vehicle for assuming it.

I did not understand then what that vehicle was. I thought it was just getting good people elected to government who would then use the people's power to act in the public interest.

But sitting in that Harlem street academy in the middle of neglected America, I could readily understand why the idea of citizen power was greeted with contempt when I raised the subject. What did that mean to these alienated young men and women? They had only to look out the window to see a street—their street—littered with debris, where crime and poverty were daily facts of life. They had no jobs, no money, nothing to call their own. What little they received from government was doled out as a privilege, not as a right. Maybe if I had talked about the possibility of getting some extra money to buy some clothes or get a car or rent a better apartment, they would have responded more enthusiastically. But "citizen power"? What was in it for them?

"Hell, man, there's no such thing as citizens around here, much less citizen power," the boy seated next to me argued. "There's just people. The only citizen I know is the dude in the White House and, I guess, maybe the fat cats that get all the money. They're the ones who call it their way. The rest of us, we got no say. We just got to cut it our own way."

"Look around you," I said. "How do you think this academy got here? It wasn't the government. A bunch of citizens joined with the Urban League to set up this academy, because so many of you were dropping out of the public school system. They couldn't get the government or the schools to come up with any solutions to the problem, so they raised the money, rented the buildings, hired the teachers, and started doing something about it on their own. I'm not saying it's going to be easy. For example, I understand the street academy program is in trouble because the private money sources are drying up and the government refuses to fill the breach by pumping in sufficient funds needed to keep it alive. That's a real shame."

Even today, in 2008, dropout rates are a significant problem. Thirty percent of our children do not graduate from high school. In many inner cities, it's considerably more.

"I guess you're right," the boy grudgingly admitted, "but that's not it, man. I mean, I'm not talking about street academies. I'm talking about the big things. You know, like going to Vietnam or getting a good job or earning more money. We don't have any say in those kinds of things."

THAT'S WHAT I WROTE IN 1971. But I could write it today about a storefront in South Chicago or Los Angeles. Sadly, the story is all too relevant 37 years later. In all that time, while many citizens have formed effective grassroots organizations to work on solving society's critical problems, the average American citizen has been precluded from the decision-making process; the disenfranchised even more so. The fact that there is so much citizen effort to make a difference and yet virtually insurmountable problems still exist in our society means that there is something drastically lacking within the system. Real power rests in the hands of those who control government by way of their investments in politicians—these politicians make the laws for those in control.

Wouldn't you rather be a part of the governing process instead of being under the thumb of those who control the government? Wouldn't you like to have enough control so that government and corporate power respond to your needs? You might argue that that takes a lot of clout. Well, how do you think business, labor, farmers or corporations are able to secure the laws that give them an edge? They do it by putting their money where their mouth is and by making sure that they get the results they want on Election Day.

People are tired of liberal "promises" and conservative "game plans" which offer the rhetoric of hope but, in reality, merely protect and perpetuate the status quo. Conservatism in America has too often meant racism and support for the wealthy against the poor. Liberalism, on the other hand, has relied too heavily on the power of the state and on faceless bureaucrats in government to solve problems, while failing to assure continued popular participation and control. The liberals have not attacked the increase and centralization of wealth and power; they have abetted it. They have sold out to Wall Street. What astounds and irritates so many people is that the liberals, both Democratic and Republican, have been in power since World War II; yet, they have not made good on their promises.

Liberals have applied some band-aid emergency measures to the poor, but their programs have been paid for by ordinary citizens, while their policies have first benefited the rich and powerful. To achieve "security" at home, they built a mighty military-industrial complex that, in turn, built a global American empire to justify it. The conservatives advanced and perpetuated it in the extreme.

Liberals also built a confusing bureaucratic structure of antipoverty and welfare programs, which robbed the middle class of their money and the poor of their incentive and integrity. These programs have been only a hodgepodge of patchwork solutions applied sporadically to meet emergencies, as Katrina revealed. Indeed, these programs have not even been able to meet the emergencies. In the first place, the real money has gone for war preparation and war making. In the second place,

4

the liberals have left the basic political and economic structure of the country untouched. Our corrupt income tax system continues to rest heavily on the middle class, and even on the poor, while it practically exempts the rich and the near-rich.

Liberal programs fostered not only great industrial growth through the military-industrial complex, the medical-industrial complex, and the security-industrial complex but also their wars—the War on Poverty, the War on Drugs, and the War on Terrorism. These programs, unfortunately, also fostered the growth of poverty, alienation and urban blight.

MOST AMERICANS TODAY are frustrated and confused. They are told by everyone that they are "the richest people in the world" and "the world's freest nation." Yet, they see poverty in the midst of plenty and continued erosion of their civil liberties. America is no longer #1 in any of the important social and economic indices of the world. In fact, the only areas in which we are #1 are weaponry; consumer spending; government, corporate and private debt; environmental pollution; energy consumption; the incarcerated men and women in our criminal justice system; and, of course, delusion. With national security as practically the only primary concern of the state since World War II, enormous portions of our wealth and human resources have been misappropriated to military programs, while desperate human needs lie neglected in every corner of our nation.

Now the people want to be empowered. This kind of empowerment strongly supports the old liberal notions of increasing the public sector and public responsibility in all areas of life, including business and work. It also supports the traditional conservative notions of freedom to be left alone and the necessity of strong protection of the individual against the state. This kind of empowerment goes beyond the authentic forms of liberalism and conservatism in the tasks it sets for itself. First, it seeks to change the present tremendous concentration of wealth and power in America. Second, it carves out new areas of autonomous public interests and forms highly visible and active citizen constituencies capable of fracturing the existing power structure.

People empowered will demand a balance of power between the citizens and their elected officials. People empowered will want the government to be an instrument of protection and action on their behalf, but—and this is the big difference—as their servant rather than as their master.

The only possibility of government reform is through empowerment of the people. This will permit the people to address those forces in society that have power to block a government responsive to their social, environmental and economic needs. Unfortunately, the people haven't come to realize that their empowerment must take the form of lawmaking—the central power of government. Anything less continues their present mendicancy. However, this concept is "out of the box" for the average citizen who is weaned on the concept that he controls government on Election Day. He hasn't reasoned that in the second or two that it takes for him to cast his vote, he gives his power away to politicians who tell him what he wants to hear to get his vote.

PEOPLE WILL HAVE TO SUFFER a level of frustration and anger sufficient to reason their way out of this conundrum and reach for an "out of the box" solution to their own empowerment. They must realize that **they** are the solution, not their leaders.

Then, they will be able to attack not only the forces that control our government, but also the ideology that supports them. When we assail the military-industrial complex, for example, we assail the idea of a system which values building missiles for overkill more than education. When we criticize business or industry, we criticize the notion that any part of the American economy can be run for private profit alone without regard for the public's interests.

The awesome creativity of people needs to be injected into the governance of the polity. The people will be able to assume the adult responsibility of citizenship necessary to preserve their own freedoms and solve society's problems. Such responsible participation furthers an open adversarial environment of ideas in keeping with the original design of American government, which generated a built-in arena of conflict through the devices of checks and balances—our separation of powers. People empowered thereby become the fourth check of our troika of existing checks and balances.

WHEN I SERVED as United States senator from Alaska, the environmentalist constituency served as adversary to the oil companies to ensure that construction of the trans-Alaska pipeline did not excessively damage the Alaskan ecology. A poorly constructed pipeline would not only have endangered the environment, it also would have raised the end cost of oil for the consumer. The nation's energy consumers needed Alaska's oil, but no one wanted a bad pipeline. Conservationists in Alaska used the 102 Statement of the National Environmental Protection Act to block construction of the oil pipeline by court injunction until the project could be proven environmentally safe.

People empowered not only will be able to set forth broad goals and general principles and make specific proposals for attaining their stated objectives, but they will also be able to enact those goals into laws. People empowered will unleash creative new solutions to old problems.

The next chapters discuss some of the major problems facing Americans today and the ways in which people empowered as lawmakers, working in tandem with their elected legislators at every level of governance, can more effectively address these problems.

The major thrust of this book is to define how American citizens can become empowered as legislators through the enactment of the National Initiative, a federal ballot initiative which will for the first time in our history define our ability to govern ourselves with a government "by the people."

Citizens Are the Solution

The optimism of grassroots movements raises false expectations.

False expectations create new generations of cynics.

A citizen gives his power away on Election Day to politicians.

The central power of government is lawmaking.

For people to control government, they must become lawmakers.

Empowered people are able to make laws in partnership with their elected representatives.

Enactment of the National Initiative for Democracy—a federal ballot initiative—will serve as the vehicle to empower people to become lawmakers.

2

The National Initiative for Democracy

The basis of our political systems
is the right of the people to make and to alter
their constitutions of government.
George Washington
1787

More than half of American citizens have been making laws by initiative at the state and local levels of government for the last hundred years. A close examination of the people's legislative record in the 24 states and numerous local communities shows they have legislated responsibly and many times more so than their elected legislators, particularly on fiscal matters; and this was done without the deliberative legislative procedures that exist in all legislative bodies. Civil service, old-age assistance (a precursor to Social Security), campaign finance reform, term limits and women's right to vote are a few examples of progressive legislation initiated by the people.

These state initiative laws were enacted in the late 19th and early 20th Centuries by populists and progressives, permitting voters to make laws at the state and local levels of government. Unfortunately, those reformers failed to enact deliberative legislative procedures or create an administrative agency to keep the people's legislative activities independent from the officialdom of representative government. As a result, state and local officials, jealous of their power, are able to thwart the people's legislative process and deny them the full and unfettered use of initiative laws.

The representative system of government structurally maintains citizens in civic adolescence. Proof of this exists in the passive acceptance by the people of the ridiculous actions of their elected legislators and their administrative officials. These government leaders decide to go to war and then refuse to raise taxes to pay for the war. Worse still, they cut taxes, passing the financial burden on to our grandchildren. I could cite further proof with respect to education, Social Security, healthcare, taxation, the War on Drugs, trade, energy, and environmental policy. It's embarrassing to then see politicians promoting this behavior with a straight face.

WHEN PEOPLE GIVE their political power away on Election Day, they then hold their representatives responsible for public policy decisions even though they, the voters, are responsible for electing those representatives. Ultimately, responsibility always rests with the people. The present structure of representative government denies the people the opportunity to take responsibility for public policy decisions and their consequences, thereby limiting their ability to mature civically. Consider the family structure: Parenting teaches us that we raise our children to adulthood by paying out responsibility to them over time, teaching them to face life and become responsible for their actions.

The structural flaws of representative government are not self-correcting. Thomas Jefferson described the problem in a letter to Edward Carrington in 1787.

> If once [the people] become inattentive to the public affairs, you and I, and Congress and assemblies, Judges and Governors, shall all become wolves. It seems to be the law of our general nature, in spite of individual exceptions.

The watershed period, at the turn of the 20th Century, enacting initiative laws primarily in western states, was a reaction to the extreme corruption of our elected officials by business and corporate interests—capitalism. This era of citizen empowerment ended with the First World War. War restrictions under the Wilson Administration enabled corporate elites to regain control of the polity and stem the tide of citizen empowerment. I expand upon this subject in Chapter 12.

Our elected representatives are human beings; it is in their nature to wield the people's political power to protect and expand their own self-interest, that of their financial and political backers who helped them to secure and maintain their offices, and that of the political party to which they belong and in which they share power. Human nature and the natural corrupting influence of power are hardly correctable by those who profit from it. The people, empowered as lawmakers, are the only possible corrective force.

For democracy to work, the people not only must be informed, but must also be empowered to act upon that information. Raising people's expectations that they can influence government and their representatives to deal with the public interest induces apathy when those expectations prove to be illusory. Many, especially the younger generation who opt out of any role in politics, seem to be the more intelligent in refusing to try over and over something they perceive as not working. This is compounded by the natural tendency of politicians to sell hope without substance, thereby promoting cynicism.

Pundits and students of government generally agree that our federal government is dysfunctional—with the Congress in gridlock, an imperial presidency steeped in its own hubris, and a judiciary anointed with papal powers for life. Conventional wisdom informs us that our government under the Bush Administration is the worst we have ever seen. Not so. We are captivated by the myth of "the good old days." The good old days never existed. We have selective memory about our triumphal past and amnesia about the wrongs perpetrated in each decade since our nation's founding.

We are a great people because we are stewards of a land blessed by geographic location, abundant natural resources, and the amalgam of racially and culturally diverse immigrant populations. We need to reject the arrogance of national triumphalism and appreciate our blessings—not as recognition of our worth, but as a gift from all who came before us. We need an ethic that marries the strength of our individualism with our common responsibilities in the constituent assembly of the people, nationally and globally.

If we are to grow and improve ourselves individually and collectively, we need to complete the structural design of human governance so ably

11

advanced by our founders. They were informed by the experiences of earlier societies, particularly Solon's concept of law in Greece and the Swiss concept of federalism.

The century of Swiss governance beginning in 1848, at the close of a three-year religious civil war, raised the possibilities of effective government to instructive heights. That poor, multi-ethnic, multi-lingual hardscrabble country, steeped in religious conflict, without natural resources, decided to adopt a constitution modeled on our own, except that the people were brought into the operation of government as lawmakers in partnership with their elected officials. Even the acclaimed Alexis de Tocqueville had serious doubts that this Swiss experiment in the union of direct and representative democracy would work.

However, the result is without precedent in human history. Switzerland, living in peace, has evolved into the most successfully governed and on a per capita basis one of the wealthiest nations in the world. Its only distinguishing feature from all other democracies in the world is the involvement of its people as lawmakers within the operations of government.

THE UNITED STATES OF AMERICA is not, in fact, a democracy, nor are the other "democracies" of the world. They are all representative governments. In a democracy, the people are the government. In our "democracies," we elect representatives to run the government for us. Those we elect do not, for the most part, run the country first and foremost in the interest of the people; as human nature dictates, they run it for their own interests first. We are led to believe by those who control the polity that we have no choice but to give our sovereign power to politicians on Election Day.

That need not be the case!

The central power of government is lawmaking—not voting. Those who make the laws determine how, when, and if citizens can vote. Florida in 2000 and Ohio in 2004 are recent examples. Citizens can gain control of their government by becoming lawmakers, empowered to make laws for their own benefit. The people are more conservative than their elected officials, regardless of political party, particularly when it comes to limiting the continuous growth of government.

This generation of Americans must complete the work of the founders by bringing American citizens into the operations of government as lawmakers in a governing partnership with our elected officials.

Are the people qualified to make laws governing their lives? They're qualified enough at the state and local levels of government. They're qualified enough on Election Day to give their power away to political candidates who manipulate the electoral process with money from special interests to get elected. In fact, it's easier for citizens to decide on policy issues themselves rather than try to guess what representatives will do after they get in office. It's even more difficult when you realize that politicians say whatever it takes to get elected.

Do Americans want to become lawmakers? Polls show that people overwhelmingly want to be empowered. The only possible empowerment tool is lawmaking. For the last 225 years, citizens have been sold on the legislative monopoly of representative government where power is wielded by their elites.

HOW CAN AMERICANS become lawmakers? The Congress is not likely to dilute its powers by empowering the people. Therefore, the people themselves must enact a federal ballot initiative called the National Initiative for Democracy, a proposed law that my colleagues and I have developed and refined over the past decade to empower citizens as lawmakers in every government jurisdiction of the United States—in a partnership with their elected officials. The enacting process goes entirely around the U.S. government and is legal under our Constitution.

The ideological foundation of the National Initiative rests on the belief that the constituent power of the people is sovereign, and the American people—like all peoples—can govern themselves as they see fit in pursuit of their happiness and their general welfare. George Washington in 1787 said it best:

> People can decide with as much propriety on the alterations and amendments [to the Constitution] which shall be found necessary, as ourselves, for I do not conceive that we are more inspired, have more wisdom or possess more virtue than those who will come after us.

The National Initiative is a legislative package, sponsored by The Democracy Foundation (www.nationalinitiative.us), a non-profit IRS 501c(3) corporation that includes an amendment to the Constitution and a federal statute.

The Democracy Amendment (1) amends the Constitution asserting the legislative powers of the people; (2) sanctions the national election conducted by the non-profit corporation, Philadelphia II, giving Americans the opportunity to vote on the National Initiative; (3) creates an Electoral Trust (vital to maintain citizen lawmaking independent from elected representatives and to administer legislative procedures on behalf of the people) and defines the role of its trustees; and (4) outlaws the use of monies not from natural persons in initiative elections; and (5) defines the electoral threshold that must be reached for the National Initiative to become the law of the land. [See Appendix A for the full text of the Democracy Amendment.]

The Democracy Act is a proposed federal statute that (1) sets out deliberative legislative procedures (copied from Congress and other legislative bodies like the Alaska Legislature) to be used for initiative lawmaking by citizens in every government jurisdiction of the United States; and (2) defines the limited powers of the Electoral Trust that administers the legislative procedures on behalf of the people. [See Appendix B for the full text of the Democracy Act.]

It is important to understand that the National Initiative does not alter the existing structure or powers of the United States government. Rather, it adds an additional check—we, the people—to our system of checks and balances, while setting up a working partnership between the people and their elected representatives.

HOW CAN AMERICAN VOTERS amend the Constitution and enact the National Initiative if Congress will not act upon it or, more than likely would oppose it? The people, using a federal ballot initiative, can go around all three branches of government to amend the Constitution. There are only two venues within the structure of our polity where constitutions, constitutional amendments, and laws can be enacted: the people or their elected representatives in government. Herein lies the problem.

The Framers in Article VII of the Constitution wrote the "Creation Article" providing procedures for the conventions of states to ratify the Constitution, which is how our government was created. They also provided procedures for federal and state government representatives to amend the Constitution in Article V, thereby perpetuating control of government by a small minority of elites. However, the Framers failed to provide procedures for "*We, the people…[to] ordain*" alterations to the Constitution or make laws, even though they repeatedly said the people had the right to change their government as they saw fit.

> All power is originally in the People and should be exercised by them in person, if it can be done with convenience, or even with little difficulty.

That was a statement made in 1789 by James Wilson, a Scottish scholar, a signer of the Declaration of Independence and the Constitution and the prime mover in securing the rapid ratification of the Constitution in Pennsylvania. George Washington appointed him an initial Associate Justice of the Supreme Court.

The conventional wisdom among many scholars holds that Article V is the only way to amend the Constitution. Article V is how the government amends the Constitution—not how the people would do it. If the people had to use Article V to amend the Constitution, they would need permission from two-thirds of the Congress and three-fourths of the state legislatures. This would mean that we, the people (the creators of our government) would have to get permission from the representatives we elected to amend the Constitution. This logic is ludicrous. The constituent power of the people—the source of all political power—cannot be subservient to the powers it creates.

James Madison had it right when, in response to an inquiry during the Constitutional Convention, he said that the people had the power to "just do it."

> The people were in fact the fountain of all power and by resorting to them, all difficulties were got over. They could alter the constitutions as they pleased.

The people can "just do it"—directly amend the Constitution via a federal ballot initiative that goes around the government to establish a legal legislative process—the National Initiative for Democracy—that empowers the people to thenceforward act as lawmakers on the policy issues affecting their lives independent of their elected legislators.

The precedent and the basis for the people to use a federal ballot initiative to enact the National Initiative and thereby provide the people with legislative procedures to amend the Constitution and make laws is Article VII of the Constitution, which permitted our forebears in 1787 and 1788 to ratify the creation of our constitutional government. Today's communications technology permits us to use the precedent of Article VII to ask all American citizens if they wish to be empowered as lawmakers by choosing to enact the National Initiative in an electoral process that is fair, transparent and reasonable. Philadelphia II, a non-profit IRS 501c(4) corporation, is conducting just such an election on behalf of the American people to bring about for the first time in our history a national government "by the people."

Many stakeholders in the status quo perpetuate the myth that the people are not wise enough to enact laws on policies that affect their lives. Nevertheless, the people are expected to select the individuals who then make those decisions. The selection of representatives to make those decisions is considerably more difficult and made more so by the manipulations of campaigns than the people making those policy decisions directly. This myth that the people are not up to the legislative task of their own self-governance is totally discredited by the 100-year history of the people competently legislating by initiative at the state and local levels of government, and by the Swiss national experience.

Can "we, the people" amend the Constitution and make laws? Of course we can—we are the sovereigns. We need a process that is fair, transparent, and reasonable. The national ballot initiative to enact the National Initiative is more transparent than that of any representative government. The national election being conducted by Philadelphia II to enact the National Initiative under the precedent of Article VII is fair and transparent.

IF AMERICANS WISH to be empowered as lawmakers and truly have a government "by the people," they must vote at the web site, www.nationalinitiative.us. Support of the effort by tax-deductible contributions is welcome. The enactment of the National Initiative overcomes the legislative monopoly of representative government. If a majority of those who voted in the last presidential election vote for the National Initiative for Democracy—regardless of the views of those in government—it then becomes the law of the land. The legality of this process has been affirmed by constitutional scholars from a number of the nation's most prestigious universities.

The National Initiative's electoral process began on September 17, 2002, allowing people to use the Internet to vote. The successful use of this ubiquitous technology now depends on supporters networking with their friends, relatives, colleagues and organizations and informing them that citizens can be empowered to vote on all the policy issues that affect their lives by voting to enact the National Initiative.

With the enactment of the National Initiative, the American people will experience the responsibility of legislating and governing themselves directly, bringing them the benefits of greater civic maturity. Imagine what you, empowered as a lawmaker, might institute or change for the betterment of your community or country.

The National Initiative for Democracy

Permits citizens access to the central power of government—lawmaking.

Completes the work of the Constitutional Framers by providing legislative procedures for the people to amend the Constitution and make laws.

Permits the people to empower themselves, if they choose.

Allows citizens to vote on all public policies that affect their lives.

Would have allowed the U.S. to exit Iraq in 2006—in fact, it would have stopped the invasion from ever happening.

Establishes, for the first time in our history, a nation governed "by the people."

Induces greater civic maturity in people—a benefit that will inure to all the institutions of society.

3

Closing the Education Gap

Next in importance to freedom and
justice is popular education,
without which neither
freedom nor justice can be
permanently maintained.
James A. Garfield

AMERICANS HAVE ALWAYS had a love affair with education. Ask any American father and mother what they want most for their children and "a good education" invariably will be near the top of their list. It is part of our national dream of equality, the means by which the disadvantaged can achieve for themselves economic well-being and social acceptance, the stimulus for individual enrichment and achievement and the prerequisite for national advancement. It can provide the major and enduring solution for problems of crime, prejudice, and poverty.

Despite its obvious virtues, however, education today is the victim of growing criticism, some justified and some not. There is a crisis of confidence among the people in the ability of education to fulfill its role in what Horace Mann, the father of American education, termed "the great equalizer of the conditions of men." They rightly complain that education today too often is unequally dispensed, ineffectively administered, and lacking in relevancy and creative innovation. In order to strengthen education, therefore, people empowered as policy makers must demand that it be developed as a humanizing institution with a viable economic base of taxation politically sustained by citizen and elected legislators.

Education has become one of this nation's biggest businesses. Some Americans derive satisfaction from the fact that during the current school year more than 60 million people are engaged in our education enterprise as students, teachers, or administrators and that some 6% of the gross national product is spent on education. I do not find this satisfactory. We need to open the doors of education to even more Americans of all ages; we should expand the ranks of qualified teachers and administrators; we must provide additional funds for increased salaries, improved facilities, and more modern equipment; and we need to see to it that those monies are raised by a formula based on ability to pay and redistributed according to need.

I find little solace in the fact that some education is available to most young Americans. It does not disguise the imperfections of a system that often favors the haves over the have-nots and produces an ever-increasing number of teenage dropouts, while adults who may need re-training find a scarcity of educational opportunities available to them. In short, we must reevaluate the merits, and perhaps even redesign the structure, of an educational program that fails to meet the expectations of students, parents or the demands of the workforce.

Unless the existing educational system is improved sufficiently to meet the needs and demands of today's changing society, we shall have to consider the implementation of entirely new methods for dispensing education. It is generally assumed that schools are fixed and immutable. Therefore, changing the child to fit the school is the solution. I think often changing the schools would be more appropriate. Research indicates that underprivileged children do not learn well because they enter school without many of the attitudes and the linguistic, cognitive, and affective skills that are absolutely necessary for them to succeed in school. It is easy to say, then, teach them that before they come to school.

Another possibility is giving parents educational vouchers which could be used to send their children to any school of their choice, public or private, or, if they prefer, to engage in specialized education activities such as apprenticeships or study projects. The cash value of each voucher would approximate the amount spent on the education of one child each year by the local school district. Vouchers offer the flexibility and the element of individual choice so often lacking in our educational institutions today.

Teachers unions contend that vouchers would undermine the public school system by giving money earmarked for public schools to private schools. I agree that we need to devote more resources to fix our public schools—and I believe with the right political leadership we can. But in the meantime, we should help out low-income parents who want to send their children to private schools. Why should poor children suffer from the incompetence and cowardice of our political and educational leaders?

We must also understand that the failures of our educational institutions cannot be entirely blamed on a lack of funding. The malaise of a society racked by continuing racial strife, unnecessary wars, unemployment, poverty, and myriad other social and economic ills, plants the seeds, long before the student arrives in school. This often produces such deplorable educational conditions. Economic and technological changes have created new challenges and placed new demands on education. Education now must rise to the occasion.

While recognizing that education is perhaps our best long-term solution to problems, it is first necessary to understand that, paradoxically, education is also the source of many of our problems. Before the creation of the public school system, the uneducated knew only what they experienced. They were unaware that they could make life better for themselves. They could not read, and they did not socialize with people outside their socioeconomic class. It was not until schools were opened to them that they began to learn that education could offer alternatives to them. Awareness developed and a new impatience. The more men knew, the more they expected; and they did not want to wait. "The evil which was suffered patiently as inevitable seems unendurable as soon as the idea of escaping from it crosses men's minds," de Tocqueville observed. "All the abuses then removed call attention to those that remain, and they now appear more than galling. The evil, it is true, has become less, but sensibility to it has become more acute."

But educated men not only complained; they also kept busy doing other things. Some built industries that polluted the waters, automobiles that polluted the air, and buildings that blocked the sky and replaced trees and grass.

SOME OF THE BEST MINDS from the best schools created the greatest injustices. Somewhere, somehow, morality was lost; and although we now know how to do thousands of things, we have not distinguished which ones are worth doing and which are better forgotten. The purpose of machinery, we all know, is to serve man. We all must know how to make a living, but we must also learn how to live. If the schools are to teach us this, they must be made into humane institutions. The development of the complete person—his total human potential—has to be learned. Therefore, creating and maintaining a humane learning environment within the school system is critically important.

I see a humanistic school as one that accepts, even celebrates, personal differences and yet emphasizes the common qualities people share. It is one that aids the students in understanding their predecessors and in growing from them without being restricted by them. Its goal for the students is superior scholarship so that they can contribute to society while further developing their own personalities. It supplies the means for the students to mature by examining their own lives. "Men are men before they are lawyers, or physicians, or merchants, or manufacturers, and if you make them capable and sensible men, they will make themselves capable and sensible lawyers or physicians," John Stuart Mill observed in his Inaugural Address at the University of St. Andrew.

EVEN THE MOST HUMANE INSTITUTIONS require proper funding to be effective, however; and the financial inadequacies blocking full development of our educational system are appalling. The greatest offender in this regard is the federal government. While piously extolling the virtues of quality education for all Americans, the government consistently fails to put its money where its mouth is or to give the issue the priority it deserves.

According to the National Priorities Project, the $500 billion appropriated thus far for the war in Iraq could have been used to hire an additional 8,862,540 elementary school teachers or place 67,733,683 children in Head Start. We could have built 48,144 new elementary schools or given 19,832,874 scholarships to university students.

What a terrible price we are paying for the poor judgment of leaders who could not recognize that by choosing to wage an unnecessary war, they were also choosing to deprive our children of a better future.

What damning evidence this presents to prove that the public does not have the power needed to protect its interests. The public-interest rhetoric is there, in the White House and on the floors of Congress, but when the chips are down the decision makers will respond most quickly and most favorably to the special moneyed interests which helped to place them in office. This is why I insist that the election process be based on public finances rather than private contributions. Too many pre-election "contributions" are paid off with post-election "favors." Corporate elites have learned to invest in elections in anticipation of rewards. Doesn't it make more sense for the public to pay for the cost of electing officials in anticipation of rewards for the general public interest?

While the federal executive and legislative respond so generously to the pressures of the powerful military-industrial complex, state and local governments have to come up with a whopping 93% of the education price tag. Small wonder citizens at the local level find themselves economically smothered under ever-increasing property taxes which are not only economically burdensome, but are an unfair basis for financing education.

As we take steps to correct the inequities of financing education at the local level, we must also escalate our national commitment to education beyond the present 6% of our gross national product to 8%, 10%, 12% or more—whatever is needed. At least one-half of that dollar amount should be put up by the federal government. At the same time the federal government must make up whatever dollar differences are required to meet the special needs of those localities which have deficiencies in their fiscal capabilities.

There are other steps needed to achieve equal opportunity in education. State aid must be adjusted to take into account the higher costs of education in certain areas, and funds must be allocated to provide appropriate educational opportunities for children with special needs and those with special skills, including the academically gifted. I take exception, however, to the matching-fund formula or the use of special subsidies for rewarding districts which spend more money on children requiring extra attention than is usually spent on mainstreamed children. Such financial arrangements favor those affluent school districts which are better able to raise the necessary funds for such purposes. If a school district needs more money to meet the requirements of all of its students, it should be able to apply to the federal government for a subsidy. Providing matching funds or special subsidies to upper socioeconomic school districts serves only to siphon off the available funds that should be going to all or to the more needy school districts.

Of course, simply allocating more money to education is not enough. The funds must then be distributed in a manner that will do the most good, allocating grants on a basis of need, rather than according to the wealth of the school districts.

Given our current priorities, children who need education the most are often receiving the least: 30% of our students drop out before they get their high school diploma. Half of all African-American dropouts wind up in prison. We not only waste money failing to educate millions of young people, we also spend even more money locking many of them up. Let's redirect our funds to empower our young people to become productive, wage-earning, tax-paying members of society. We hear a lot about how kids today don't respect themselves and others. Give them a good education that will enable them to get jobs where they earn a good paycheck and the respect of their communities after an honest day's work—and I guarantee they will respect themselves.

THE NEEDY CHILDREN of our society are getting the short end of the stick when it comes to quality of instruction as well. It is understandable that the most experienced, best qualified teachers would usually choose to pursue their profession in the more wealthy neighborhoods. After all, that is where one finds the finest schools, the best prepared students, and the nicest and safest surroundings. Yet, it is the not-so-safe neighborhoods, the not-so-fine schools, and the not-so-advantaged students which most desperately need the specialized expertise of skilled teachers. I propose a federally supported supplementary salary program to reward those teachers who accept the added challenges of teaching in our educationally deprived areas. Surely if we can pay government workers and military personnel as much as a 25% bonus for serving in so-called "hardship" areas around the world, we can do as much for our teachers here at home. Such a program would enable financially struggling school districts to compete more favorably with their wealthier counterparts in recruiting the talent to provide the quality instruction needed by our disadvantaged youngsters.

We must also make more efficient use of our expensive educational facilities. It is ridiculous for these costly institutions to remain idle and unused for three months out of every year. The summer vacation is an archaic custom instituted by an agrarian society that needed to have its children on the farms to help with the summer and early fall harvesting. Japanese students spend 240 days in the classroom. Most European countries mandate 220 days. But our children spend 180 on average. It's no mystery why foreign students consistently beat our kids in head-to-head academic competitions. We need to extend educational opportunities.

Not only must we utilize our public educational facilities more fully, we must recognize the value of using private schools to help meet our educational goals. I see no compelling reason why private schools should not receive federal funds as long as they are primarily education-oriented, instead of religion-oriented, with the understanding, of course, that they cannot bar enrollment of any youngster because of religion, race, or economic background. The existence of parochial schools, for example, has eased the burden for many underfinanced and overpopulated school districts. This has been dramatically proven in those districts where parochial schools have been forced to shut down because of a lack of funds, and their students have suddenly been thrust into the public school system. The only criterion which should matter in qualifying for federal financial assistance is whether a school provides quality education indiscriminately and effectively.

AFTER YEARS AND YEARS of failing schools, the federal government finally woke up to the concept of accountability. Unfortunately, their solution to the lack of accountability was No

Child Left Behind, which mandates testing so "failing schools" can be identified and punished. Many politicians point to rising test scores and call that program a success. Of course, scores will rise when teachers are forced to teach to a test and dedicate their math and reading courses to teaching test-taking skills. Some principals increase time for test preparation by cutting not only art, gym and music but history and science as well. No wonder kids are bored with school. We are shaping them into good test-takers—a bunch of pleasers who lack entrepreneurial instinct, intellectual curiosity and creative thinking.

I constantly hear people complain that kids today spend too much time playing computer games and not enough playing sports. We fear our children are becoming fat, soft, nerds. Well, playing technology games is just an extension of what our education system values: acquiring a set of skills that allows you perform a rote task so you can get the highest score.

I want to introduce accountability for teachers. We all know that money is a primary motivator. However, the other Democratic presidential candidates adamantly resist rewarding great teachers with extra pay because they fear the teachers unions. Why should teachers with energy, excitement, and talent be paid the same as the ones who don't make an effort? What other profession in America protects the mediocre at the expense of excellence?

Teacher accountability is also abrogated once a teacher gains tenure. This is not to say that most teachers will not continue to provide their best efforts, but if it is important to have checks and balances outside the educational system, certainly it is as important to have them within the system. The debilitating effects of seniority ascribed to our legislative halls are no less so when found in education or anywhere else for that matter. A teacher, who is no longer effective in the classroom, whether it is because of age or ability or for any other reason, should not be able to escape accountability because of tenure alone. A method must be devised, through administrative procedures and hearings and with the end decision being taken by elected school board members (subject to the wishes of the people affected), to strike down the immunity of tenure when poor performance warrants it.

To improve the "system," teachers' attitudes have to continue to change. Teachers who think their students are incapable of learning very often find this to be true. Yet, a different teacher with the same class and a different assumption sees them become interested in learning.

I was not a very good student when I was a youngster growing up in Springfield, Massachusetts. I was a poor reader and had considerable difficulty in expressing myself clearly; I discovered years later it was because I was severely dyslexic. As a consequence, I became disinterested and unresponsive. School was something to be endured, not enjoyed; learning was a chore to be avoided.

In my senior year of high school, however, something happened that changed my attitude and my life. A remarkable and dedicated teacher, Brother Edgar Bourque, recognized my reticence as just a problem to be overcome. Because of his interest and his willingness to tutor me in speech and reading beyond the classroom demands, I discovered the joys of learning and was imbued with the desire to maximize my talents.

I have never forgotten that experience or failed to benefit from it. I was one of the fortunate ones, and I often wonder how many boys and girls will never realize their full potential because there are not enough Edgar Bourques in the teaching profession or because, for some other reason, they will receive something less than the kind of education they need to develop fully and to compete well in our society.

Well-trained teachers must and can meet the challenge and learn why students who had been lively and eagerly interested upon first entering school are quite bored by the time they reach fifth grade. This is especially true in lower-income schools, although it is hardly absent in higher-income ones. It is time to make education more exciting, more interesting, and purposeful. Curricula that fail to satisfy and excite students must be studied and revised or replaced with imagination and daring. Details are only steppingstones to understanding concepts which are of fundamental importance. Teachers must know their subjects well enough to reach their students in creative ways and relate academic content to their students' educational goals.

BOREDOM IS THE GREATEST CURSE of our educational system. We are wasting the time of millions of our children, and they know it. We need to think outside of the box to stop wasting huge amounts of time and money. Kids are different than they were 30 years ago. They reach puberty earlier and are exposed to so much information at younger ages that it doesn't make sense to maintain the traditional 12-year academic track. We need to start schooling children earlier, allowing them to enter higher education or obtain technical training earlier, and getting them into the workforce sooner. Parents should have the option of preschool programs for their children. Students should have longer school days and academic years, with the availability of tutoring and supervised study periods.

High school should end at 16 for those who meet graduation requirements. All college-bound students should be given tuition assistance, if needed. Those who don't want to attend college should receive publicly funded technical training. Programs are needed in high school to help students measure their aptitudes, interests and abilities; too few schools offer these programs. Tax breaks should be given to companies that hire and train teenagers to perform technology-based jobs. The right way to fight outsourcing of jobs is not by erecting trade barriers but by preparing our youth to compete.

One of the most glaring inequities in our present approach toward education is the exclusion from the continuing education process of millions of working Americans who do not have the financial resources or the available time. Trapped in a work-a-day environment, the education of most adults virtually comes to a halt while elsewhere new discoveries are made, new information is acquired, and new educational techniques are perfected. This is unfair to the individual and wasteful for society.

Adult education has to be expanded for low income workers who want to boost their earning power, people with high incomes returning to school simply for the pleasure of learning, and people who need further education for various licenses and apprenticeships.

Better educated people make better citizens and better workers. Therefore, I propose that every American worker be afforded the opportunity to avail himself of a year's educational sabbatical leave once every 10 years. The individual could then elect either to enhance his formal education or job skills through classroom study and specialized training programs, broaden his knowledge and cultural awareness through travel, devote his time to help correct a social ill by working with the poor, the sick, and the disadvantaged, or, if he prefers, rejuvenate his mental and physical capabilities through rest and relaxation. The totally educated man, after all, is not the product of the classroom alone; he is the sum of his experiences and activities at all levels of society.

The concept of educational sabbaticals is not new. Teachers periodically are granted time off to travel and otherwise acquire fresh understanding and information which can be translated into more effective and meaningful classes in the schoolroom. Industry and government, too, recognize the value of continually upgrading the performance and the worth of selected employees by sending them to colleges and universities so they can keep abreast of improved management procedures and technological developments.

Eligibility for the sabbatical would be automatic for any person who has worked a total of 10 years and would renew itself every 10 years thereafter. A person's qualifying time would not be limited to the number of years spent in any one job, but would be accumulated and transferred with the worker if and when he changed positions. A potential employer, in this way, would know when the employee's sabbatical would take effect and could plan for a temporary replacement or a re-juggling of responsibilities and duties needed to fill the gap caused by the worker's absence. Instead of asking whether any individual's military service obligation has been met, the employer would want to know when his sabbatical is due.

Imagine the benefits to be accrued to the economy alone. Thousands of sabbatical workers each year would travel, enroll in schools, and engage in new activities. They would stimulate increased services, buy new products, and spend money in different places. It could only mean more jobs and a more viable economy. Most importantly, however, it would provide continuing educational opportunities for all ages and at all levels.

America's Failure in Education

One third of our children fail to graduate from high school, thereby being condemned to a sub-economic existence.

Our children must be trained for adulthood with a year-around academic system with a minimum of at least 200 classroom days.

We must create safe and humane environments in all schools.

Teachers should be paid as professionals and be expected to work year round, with merit pay for excellence and the system of tenure reexamined.

Competitive and alternate forms of education should be made available through vouchers or others forms of equitable distribution of the educational dollar.

The real estate base of educational funding should be re-examined.

The federal government should pay more than 50% of the cost of education and establish standards and curriculum accordingly.

Education should be made available to adults to become better qualified for their life's work and to culturally enrich their lives.

The nation's educational goals should be equal to that of Finland, Sweden, Spain and a number of other nations which educate their children from childhood to the highest level at public expense.

If Americans are to succeed in a competitive world and enjoy a rewarding life, they need something better than a 20th Century educational system in a cybernated 21st Century.

4

Tax Reform – The Fair Tax

Taxation WITH representation ain't so hot either.
Gerald Barzan

In examining the imbalances in our present economy, the single greatest deficiency is in the distribution of income and wealth. Politicians and corporate spokespersons are fond of saying that our economy is creating more affluence for more people than ever before. However, numerous studies have shown that the distribution of income and wealth has remained virtually unchanged for the past 75 years. Since 1910, the richer half of the population has claimed three-quarters of national personal income while the poorer half has had to get along on the remaining one-quarter. Today, the richest one-fifth of our citizens commands fully 42% of the personal income, while the lower three-fifths combined receive 31%. And if we look at the richest 5%, we find that they take 17% of all the income, while the bottom 40% of the population gets only 15%.

The pattern of the distribution of wealth—the ownership of America—is even more inequitable. Currently it is estimated that less than 2% of the people own 32% of the prime wealth of the nation. They own almost 100% of the tax-free municipal and state bonds, 80% of the stock in corporations, and more than 50% of the unincorporated business assets—all sources of revenue, which increase their wealth.

Ownership for the so-called affluent middle class is largely confined to their homes (most of which are mortgaged and therefore partly owned by banks) and their personal possessions, a good number of which also have shared ownership with the bank, credit union or finance company. Less than two out of 10 families own businesses, stocks and bonds, and other income-producing assets. The bottom half of the population holds only 10% of the wealth, and a great many own nothing.

As life expectancy has risen, insufficient resources have been set aside for retirement income, and the result has created a crisis in our pension system. There is nothing worse than working your entire career, comfortable in the knowledge that a portion of your income has been safely tucked away for your retirement, only to have the rug pulled out from under you when you are forced out of your job or when the company goes under, causing you to lose your pension in the process. This problem is affecting more and more people today.

It has always been the goal of progressives to use the tax system to correct the disparity among America's rich, the middle, and the poor. Attempts to spread the largesse of the economy more evenly in society by how the government raises revenue—our income tax and inheritance tax system—have failed. Since there is no talk of serious tax reform, it is obvious there is no will in Congress to revisit the progressive goals of yesteryear. Our last hope for progressive tax reform was the Democratic Party, but it was hijacked and delivered to Wall Street during the Clinton Administration, where it is now in residence along with the Republican Party.

Wealthy Americans have played the system to their advantage and will always be able to maintain their advantage because of wealth. Wealth continually exerts its influence on government to create even more tax loopholes, guaranteeing that the wealthy will continue to pay proportionately less in taxes than the rest of the population. Moreover, since wealth controls the economy, it is able to compensate for loss of income through taxes by raising prices and the profits of business enterprises. They also influence government to return a good part of the tax money in corporate subsidies.

I served on the Senate Finance Committee (the tax writing committee) for eight years. To understand why the Congress cannot correct our tax dilemma, let me share with you a conversation I had with the chairman, Senator Russell Long, the son of Huey Long of

Louisiana lore. At the end of my first year on the committee, I went to Russell to complain of our corrupt income tax system and to present a plan I had developed for a single tax, a plan with many similarities to the tax plan I now propose. He derided my plan by pointing out that I didn't understand how things worked in Congress.

My plan would have diluted the power of the Finance Committee and the Congress by removing the ability of the Congress to create incentives in the national economy to accomplish certain social goals by providing tax credits, deductions, rapid write-offs, and other enticements. He boasted that our Finance Committee was considerably more powerful than the Appropriations Committee in that our committee could appropriate the wealth of the nation's economy through the tax system while the Appropriations Committee could only appropriate the revenues of the government. Besides he added, "How would we take care of our friends if we gave up that power?"

I HOLD THE VIEW that Congress will never correct our inequitable tax structure because at its core, the existing tax system is about getting and keeping power, stupid. At the time, I wrote about my single tax plan in the original tax chapter of *Citizen Power* back in 1971; that chapter is now replaced by the present text.

The main function of government is to raise revenue without which there is no government. When government raises revenue unfairly, the taxpayers know intuitively that the revenues funding government programs will also be allocated unfairly. This creates abhorrence of taxation and an aversion to allocating the revenue that is vital to the health and safety of the nation.

There is only one way to assure equitable taxation, and that is simplicity with total transparency. Make it so everyone knows precisely what he is paying and what everyone else is paying. Make it easy and efficient for the government to enforce and thereby guarantee to all citizens that everyone is contributing her or his fair share.

In my opinion, the best way to correct our corrupt tax system, with its intricate latticework of tax advantages for the wealthy, is through the total repeal of our income tax system and the elimination of the

Internal Revenue Service that administers it. We must then replace the income tax with a federal retail sales tax—the Fair Tax—directly administered by the Treasury Department. There must be no exemptions or deductions of any kind for anyone. We should have one simple, easy-to-understand tax system that is fair and that removes all loopholes and incentives for evasion.

We have played around with the federal tax structure for too long under the illusion of reforming it, using cosmetic rhetoric to get politicians through one more election. The tax code is woefully complex, incredibly wasteful, horribly inequitable, an administrative nightmare, and designed to discourage work and saving. All the tax system does now is encourage people with money to hire accountants, financial experts, tax lawyers and lobbyists to escape what they should be paying. Besides fostering a huge tax industry, it also requires huge administrative and enforcement costs. The cost to the private sector of complying with our tax code exceeds $270 billion a year. This is approximately half the treasure we squandered in the Iraq war over the last four years—a cost that is imposed on the private sector of our economy every year.

All income taxes on individuals and corporations would be repealed under the Fair Tax. Liberals bristle at the thought of relieving corporations of income taxes. Unfortunately, liberals have forgotten their lessons from Economics 101 and are fooled into thinking that by taxing corporations they shift the cost of government from the people to corporations. Corporations do not pay taxes; they merely collect taxes from their consumers for the government. In fact, a corporate tax is a disguised retail sales tax that is paid by the only single payer in our system—the one and only citizen consumer taxpayer.

The corporate tax does not, in fact, reduce the income which the holders of corporate stock receive in dividends. In an era when the major corporations can adjust prices to ensure any margin of profit return they wish, they simply take the tax into account as an added cost of production, no matter at what level it is set, and adjust their prices accordingly. As the *Wall Street Journal* observed, the tax is "treated by the corporations as merely another cost which they can pass on to their customers." In fact, close examination of the tangled corporate tax structure shows it only serves to inflate the cost of goods and services to consumers. This, in turn, cripples the competitive abilities of American enterprise when competing with corporations in other nations that raise revenues by other means. Obviously, if we eliminated all corporate taxes and subsidies, the ordinary taxpayer would come out far ahead.

The federal tax code now runs over 17,000 pages. The system is so complex that no one can fully understand its provisions, distortions, or the degree to which it is redistributing wealth across Americans of different generations and with different economic resources.

The tax system is geared in many ways to take from the poor and young and give to the rich and old. The latter are more inclined to vote on Election Day, a fact that is not lost on the Congress, which sustains our present tax mess. The shift in recent years to taxing dividends and capital gains at a 15% rate is a good example. Most U.S. equity is held by those over the age of 50. Lowering the effective tax rate on the incomes of this demographic group leaves a bigger burden on everyone else, primarily young people and families struggling to raise and educate their children.

FUNDAMENTAL TAX REFORM via the Fair Tax will bring about a system that is simple, efficient, equitable, transparent, and growth-oriented. The Fair Tax combines a federal retail sales tax plus a monthly tax rebate to each household based on its demographic composition to reimburse for the sales tax that will be paid that month when purchasing the essentials of life—food, lodging, clothing, medicine and transportation. The value of these essentials will be calculated to reflect these costs at the federal poverty level or above with the same household demographics.

The tax rebate, as well as other key features, makes the Fair Tax highly progressive: the more you spend the more you pay—as long as there are no exceptions. The income tax—the more you earn the more you pay—is similarly progressive in theory, but it has been corrupted in practice by Congress legislating exception after exception that then permits wealth to game the system.

The Fair Tax rate applies only to new goods and services. It will raise the same revenue raised by the personal income tax, the corporate income tax, the payroll (FICA) tax, and the healthcare taxes. The object of reform is to bring about fairness not to raise or lower the revenue the government presently receives. In contrast to the original Fair Tax proposal, developed by FairTax.org, I would retain the estate and gift tax to enhance tax progressivity. I would also retain existing federal excise taxes and, indeed, I would seek to enact an additional major federal excise tax on carbon.

Conventional wisdom suggests that taxing sales is regressive. Most economists disagree. They view a retail sales tax (ignoring any rebate) as neutral (proportional is their term) with respect to the treatment of the rich and the poor. Their reasoning runs like this. Whatever current and future economic resources—wealth, labor income, pension income, and others—we own or will acquire will ultimately be spent by us or our heirs on consumption. So taxing consumption at a fixed rate is equivalent to taxing these resources at the same rate.

Consequently, the ratio of tax payments to resources is always the same, making the sales tax burden proportional to resources. This proportionality of the tax burden to resources is why economists say a sales tax is neither progressive nor regressive, but rather proportional.

Economists call the tax on economic resources an *effective* tax rate. The effective rate is the one to remember in thinking about the Fair Tax. It's the one that's directly comparable to the much higher total effective resource tax rates most workers, but not most wealthy people, face under our existing system of payroll plus personal income plus corporate income taxation.

Note that under our current tax system, we don't tax wealth at all. But our current system does tax wages, in spades! And the wage tax that hits most workers the hardest is the FICA payroll tax, which is highly regressive.

The current system taxes wages, in large part regressively, but fails to tax wealth, either directly or indirectly. Yes, the current system taxes income earned on wealth, but much of this income is taxed at very low capital gains and dividend rates.

Moving from our current tax system, which is regressive when viewed from the perspective of taxing total remaining lifetime economic resources, to a sales tax is a highly progressive move because it takes us from a regressive tax system to a neutral (proportional) one, which in lay terms is really made progressive by including the monthly rebate of the tax that would be paid on the essentials of life.

What I'm proposing goes beyond simply the elimination of regressivity in the effective taxation of all economic resources, including wealth. I'm proposing a tax system that combines a proportional sales tax with a highly progressive tax rebate, which would leave us with a truly progressive, equitable tax structure that will diminish the huge disparity between the rich and the poor, thereby nurturing democracy.

HOW DO WE BRING ABOUT this progressive tax system? First, we eliminate our present regressive income tax system.

Second, we set up a federal sales tax that will effectively tax all resources—wealth as well as wages: When the rich spend their wealth and when workers spend their wages, they will both pay sales taxes. By broadening the effective tax base to include the corpus of wealth, not just the income earned on it (much of which is currently exempted or taxed at a low rate), one can lower the required resource tax rate and, thereby, reduce the tax burden on workers.

Third, thanks to the rebate, poor and average American households would pay no sales taxes in net terms; i.e., yes, they would pay taxes on their purchases of new products and services, but their monthly rebate check would compensate, and for the very poor more than compensate, them for their prospective tax payments. This method may seem convoluted but to permit exceptions at the store opens the floodgates to game the system—a process where middle-income Americans and the poor always lose.

Fourth, the current corporate income tax may seem like a tax that hits the rich. It doesn't. It's a tax that hits American consumers and workers because capital can move easily throughout the world. When capital leaves our shores, our workers end up with less capita, fewer jobs, and lower wages. The higher the U.S. corporate tax, the less capital there is in our country and the lower the real wages of U.S. workers. In eliminating the corporate income tax, the Fair Tax will eliminate a tax that sounds like it's falling on the wealthy, but is actually borne, in the main, by lower- and middle-income workers. Political demagogues blame outsourcing for a loss of jobs rather than focusing on our tax system, which is the real culprit.

Fifth, the poor elderly, living on Social Security, would end up better off. They would receive the sales tax rebate even though the purchasing power of their Social Security benefits would remain unchanged thanks to Social Security's automatic cost-of-living adjustment.

THE ESTIMATED TAX RATE of the Fair Tax is based on a recent exhaustive study by leading economists. The revenue-neutral sales tax rate, measured on an effective resource tax basis, is 23%. This rate is considerably lower than the total effective wage-tax rate most workers face on their labor earnings under our current tax system, which can be as high as 47%. Ignoring the rebate, the proposed new system would effectively tax the wealth of the rich and the wages of workers all at a 23% effective rate because both wealth and wages are resources used to purchase consumption.

Economists who have researched the possible effects of a Fair Tax predict an economic growth factor on the order of 10%. This will result in a phenomenal growth in employment opportunities as a result of investment capital pouring into the U.S. economy from all over the world since; in effect, the U.S. economy will become the largest tax haven in the world. Assuming presidential leadership capable of reordering the war-mongering priorities of the military-industrial complex, this new prosperity could fund education as the nation's top priority, provide quality healthcare for all Americans, electrify our national and urban transportation systems, rebuild the nation's crumbling physical infrastructure, remove our dependency on carbon energy and address all facets of climate change.

Having a single, transparent tax will go a very long way toward limiting federal spending growth. The reason is that everyone will suddenly realize that extra spending on anything means higher taxes on everyone. The federal retail sales tax would enhance generational and intergenerational equity by asking rich and middle class older Americans to pay taxes when they spend their wealth.

A sales tax will capture revenue presently leaking out of the system—foreign visitors to the U.S., and foreign students. These two groups make use of federal, state and local governmental facilities, yet they do not pay into the system through income tax. The value of these untaxed expenditures is enormous; foreign visitors to the U.S. and foreign students spent $23 billion in 2006. Under the Fair Tax, the U.S. would have received over $5 billion from this potential revenue source.

The same situation occurs for groups that illegally do not pay taxes, but it's more like a torrent than a leak. The normal criminal elements—drug traffickers, prostitution, and gambling of all sorts—represent hundreds of billions in taxes that go uncollected by the IRS. However, these elements in the cash economy are some of the most conspicuous spenders in society that will now be caught in the net of a consumer tax.

The Fair Tax has an unusual green component in that it discourages the production of new goods in favor of old, refurbished, secondhand products, which are not taxed when sold under the Fair Tax.

One sports fan drove home the very visible inequity of the present tax system when he complained that sitting in his *after-tax* bleacher seat and looking up at the skyboxes, he sees the wealthy and connected enjoying drinks and food and the sport spectacular in the comfort of a climate-controlled skybox all of which is paid for with *pretax* dollars.

The U.S. government is suffering a $50-$60 trillion fiscal gap. I know of no way a president or the Congress can correct that problem short of a fundamental change in our tax structure. Politicians are not wont to impose painful solutions on the public. The great benefit of the Fair Tax will be to turn our nation away from excessive consumption to saving, the effect of which will automatically address the government fiscal gap. The prosperity and jobs that will result from the projected economic growth will raise substantially the revenues of government from the Fair Tax on the purchases of goods and services to meet the growth demands of a restructuring economy. The fiscal gap will be met with current revenues. The explosive medical costs would now be paid by a percentage of the sales tax.

In my opinion, we will not be able to properly address any of our domestic problems until we solve the fiscal mess and reform our corrupt income tax system. My pessimism is compounded by the fact that I do not think the Congress is capable of reforming the tax system. It would dilute their power.

The only solution is found in Chapter 2, which outlines how the people can empower themselves to make the changes and bring about the reforms that would benefit their lives.

The Fair Tax

Abolishes the federal personal and corporate income tax, FICA, health taxes and the IRS.

Establishes a federal retail sales tax, estimated at 23%, with a universal rebate paid monthly to all registered households, regardless of income on what will be paid when purchasing the essentials of life—food, lodging, clothing, medicine, transportation, etc.

Improves incentives to work and save by taxing consumption.

Makes our revenue system totally transparent.

Allows every American to keep his or her entire paycheck and still receive his or her rebate.

Raises the same amount of revenue as the current system with much lower marginal rates.

Promotes economic growth and substantial wage increases for working Americans.

Stops the export of American jobs.

Enables people to invest their money without paying any taxes on what it earns.

5

A Healthcare Security System

For every social wrong there must be a remedy.
But the remedy can be nothing less than
the abolition of the wrong.
Henry George

A NUMBER OF YEARS AGO IN ANCHORAGE, during a political campaign, I knocked on the door of a retired plumber, a man who had worked hard all his life and who now lived in an expensive trailer with his wife. He had an automobile and a pickup truck with a camper and was obviously proud of his independence. He was enjoying the fruits of his lifelong labor. While we talked he raised the subject of medicine and how he was against providing free care to anyone and proved his point by announcing that he was a Republican voter. He said everybody should pay for his own health needs, observing "socialized medicine is bad stuff."

About a year later I happened to be in the neighborhood and, hearing the plumber's wife had died recently, paid him another call. When he opened the door, I was shocked. From a robust Alaskan in his mid-sixties he had turned into a despondent old man. And then he told me how his wife had contracted cancer and how he had used up all his financial resources to ease her suffering. The bank account was empty. He had mortgaged the trailer and sold the pickup truck and camper. One illness had wiped him out.

I've never been able to forget that man's face. It made me sad and angry—angry because it was such a senseless, mindless penalty to pay on top of his grief. And I am angrier still at how commonplace this sort of outrage is in our society and how we tolerate it. We are allowing sickness to literally wreck the lives of millions of people—the average citizen and the poor alike—by putting the cost of proper care out of reach.

Our country faces three terrible and worsening healthcare crises. First, 47 million Americans, including 8 million children, have no health insurance coverage. In 1987, the uninsured totaled 32 million. Thus, in two decades we've seen almost a 50% rise in those without health insurance.

Second, Medicare and Medicaid costs threaten to bankrupt the country. Today's elderly are now receiving, on average, over $15,000 per year from these programs. When all 77 million baby boomers are fully retired, the average benefit will exceed $25,000 measured in today's dollars. If benefit growth is not restrained, then the two programs' inflation-adjusted annual costs will run close to $1.5 trillion. These huge pending annual healthcare costs are largely responsible for the roughly $50 trillion fiscal gap separating projected future federal expenditures and receipts, where all of these amounts are valued in the present (measured in present value). This fiscal gap provides the true measure of our nation's indebtedness because it puts all future obligations, implicit and explicit, on an equal footing. Fifty trillion dollars is enormous, even in an economy as large as ours. It goes well beyond anything the nation can pay, particularly if it squanders its treasure on excessive defense spending and unnecessary wars.

The third healthcare crisis involves enormous healthcare obligations facing employers, many of whom are drowning in healthcare bills. General Motors, for instance, is sitting on more than a $50 billion healthcare liability for 73,000 employees and nearly 270,000 retirees that may ultimately spell its bankruptcy. How could GM have predicted that healthcare costs would have grown three times faster than inflation in 40 years?

The three crises are interconnected and therefore cannot be solved individually. Employers are reacting to the high cost of healthcare by eliminating their health plans. This is swelling the ranks of the uninsured. In 2000, 66% of non-elderly Americans were covered by employer-based health insurance. Today's figure is 59%. Employers that continue to offer health insurance are asking their employees to pay for ever larger shares of the premiums. Millions of U.S. workers are saying, "No, thank you" and declining coverage in their employers' plans.

As the uninsured run out of funds to cover their healthcare bill, more and more end up at the emergency room on Medicaid. Since 2000, Medicaid enrollments have soared by 35%! And, to close the circle, the fee-for-service reimbursement system used by Medicare and, to a lesser extent by Medicaid, has contributed significantly to the overall rise in the price of healthcare and, consequently, to the healthcare costs employers now face.

Most healthcare plans suggested by presidential candidates address only one of our three healthcare problems—the 47 million uninsured. Tragically these "solutions" compound the problem by mandating that businesses either cover their employees or pay an employer tax to cover them. This is forcing a failed solution that already cripples America's competitive ability abroad.

One would have thought the General Motors' experience would have been instructive to these presidential wannabes. The GM solution, creating a voluntary employees' beneficiary association (VEBA), a trust with a corpus funded by GM but controlled and operated by the UAW, merely puts off the day of reckoning for union members. Without VEBA, GM would likely be forced into Chapter 11, where more than likely the retirees would lose a considerable portion of their healthcare benefits. The UAW is gambling that the cost of healthcare will not exceed the earning and the corpus of the trust. A poor gamble in view of the Caterpillar and Detroit Diesel trusts' bankruptcies.

VEBA is viewed as a model for American industry. In my opinion, if this model is acted upon it will spell the death knell of what modest resurgence the American labor movement is enjoying in this election cycle. Thirty years ago, I argued with labor leaders that their primary focus should be on capital ownership for their members rather than the pursuit of wages and benefits. Dues and pension fund management were too strong an elixir for my arguments that also included predictions of union decline. As a strong supporter of the labor movement, which has done so much for the well-being of average Americans, I am distressed by my own analysis.

Those political candidates who suggest a Medicare single-payer system for all seem not to have noticed that the government's present managing of Medicare and Medicaid is exploding the government debt, contributing substantially to the fiscal gap. As pointed out earlier, there is only one single payer—it's not the government—it's the citizen, the taxpayer or the consumer; we can all identify with one of those roles.

In the Massachusetts plan, attractive to a number of candidates, citizens not covered by employers must purchase health insurance, a thinly disguised open-ended subsidy to the insurance industry. The uninsured get stuck in what is best described as a loser's insurance pool in which participants receive third-rate insurance coverage, thanks to significant co-payments, high deductibles, exclusions and ceilings on coverage. Since this population has much higher-than-average expected healthcare costs, the insurance companies will provide coverage only if they are compensated at a higher price than they would charge the general population.

To finance this higher price, these plans propose direct government subsidization, as well as forcing all employers who don't provide health insurance coverage to pay a special fee per worker. Those uninsured who don't work, including many very poor people, will be required to buy a health insurance policy.

It's time for a reality check. Worsening Medicaid's finances and letting Medicare hemorrhage further will leave no money for anything else, let alone massive government subsidies for losers' insurance. And, rather than help employers exit the health insurance business, the schemes permanently trap *all* employers in it. Worse yet, they may suggest to employers that they dump their plans and simply pay the losers' insurance tax for all their workers, lest the government pass a law that compels them to indefinitely maintain their very expensive current plans.

As for forcing the uninsured poor to pay for their own coverage, good luck. There is no way to force someone who is poor to buy health insurance, meaning we'll still end up with huge numbers of uninsured showing up at emergency rooms.

THE HEALTHCARE SECURITY SYSTEM (HSS), the plan I propose, provides a single solution for all three of our crises and provides quality healthcare for all Americans. It is designed to replace all state healthcare plans, employer-based healthcare systems, and eventually Medicare and Medicaid, which would be allowed to expire.

The plan provides each American, annually, with a health insurance certificate based upon his or her recent healthcare history; an unforeseen catastrophic event will be totally covered. Those with higher expected healthcare costs (the poor) receive bigger certificates. Participants use their certificate, each year, to purchase a basic health insurance policy from one of five private insurance plans or a government Medicare type plan. The plans are exactly the same, so the companies will compete not on the services provided but based on who can provide the administrative costs most efficiently. Participants can change their plan annually but cannot be dropped by the plan provider for any reason.

A National HSS Board and Regional HSS Boards (not unlike the Federal Reserve System) will first secure the computerization of each American's medical history when they sign up for their certificate. The HSS boards will be composed of healthcare stakeholders: citizens, doctors, nurses, holistic health care providers, nutritionists, educational and research institutions and representatives from the pharmaceutical and insurance industries and private care facilities.

The HSS boards will define the medical standards and the care that all plans will be required to offer, including catastrophic care. The basic plans will cover drugs, dental, eye glasses, home healthcare by family or other person, mental healthcare and nursing home and hospice care.

The boards will develop health improvement programs and individual incentives to certificate holders to minimize overuse or waste of services. The plans will compete for participants by offering incentives to improve healthier lifestyles—exercise, weight reduction, cessation of smoking, gym memberships, and other incentives to improve the nation's health.

The cost of HSS will be paid for by a percentage of the retail sales tax on all new products and services—the Fair Tax. The HSS boards will fix the total annual healthcare certificate budget for the nation as a percentage of GDP so that the nation can't go broke due to healthcare expenditures. This budgetary process is not unlike what a family or a business would reasonably impose upon itself. Obviously the HSS boards would be making triage decisions with respect to the services provided relative to age and lifestyle.

The best part of HSS is that it requires very little new financing, except for the upfront cost of computerizing every certificate recipient's health history. Total everything federal and state governments now shell out directly and indirectly via tax breaks on healthcare and throw in some significant administrative savings, and you arrive at roughly the same cost of our present broken system.

In addition to resolving three terrible problems, HSS is highly progressive. It eliminates huge tax breaks to the rich and provides certificates based on medical condition; and the poor are advantaged on average, since they are in much worse physical shape than the rich.

Finally, HSS will preserve and, indeed, will greatly strengthen our competitive healthcare industry. Individuals will have free choice of doctors, hospitals and caregivers. Certificate holders will be free to purchase additional insurance coverage if they so desire. What I'm proposing is that we redirect our current healthcare's explicit and implicit expenditures to a new system that is efficient and equitable and that won't break the bank. The retail sales tax that will pay for the system can be a portion of the Fair Tax I propose in Chapter 4.

Fourteen years have passed since our nation last seriously debated healthcare reform. Why is the issue once again front and center? The reason is clear. Our healthcare system has become so bad that it's made everyone sick—sick with fear. Forty-seven million uninsured Americans are living day to day, scared to death that they'll get sick and have to hand over their life savings to pay their medical bills. Millions of insured workers live with the gnawing fear that they could be next— next to lose their employer's insurance coverage because the business can no longer carry the cost. And millions of elderly go to bed at night worrying whether Medicare is running short of money, whether they'll be able to afford Medicare's soaring premiums, whether their doctors will drop them because of Medicare's low reimbursement rates, and, heaven forbid, whether they will end up like so many others—living in a nursing home, flat broke, and at the mercy of Medicaid.

Our current system stinks. There's no other way to put it. And suddenly, everybody but everybody seems to realize it. To me the parameters for change are clear. To reiterate, we need a single, efficient, transparent system that includes everyone, that treats everyone fairly, that covers all the basics, including prescription drugs, home healthcare, and nursing home care, and that costs no more than the economy can afford.

In sum, I believe the time is ripe for a broad healthcare compact. But achieving this compact will require every American to think outside his or her current healthcare box and examine the HSS plan I propose.

Healthcare Security System

Gives quality healthcare coverage to all Americans.

Provides each American, annually, with a health plan certificate.

Offers certificates of larger value for those with higher expected healthcare costs.

Offers participants free choice of doctors, hospitals, and caregivers.

Offers participants choice of insurance or government plans.

Defines standards and services for the plans through the National and Regional HSS Boards.

Covers such services as drugs, dental, eye glasses, home healthcare, nursing home care, etc.

Fosters competition between plans for participants based on preventive care and efficient administrative costs.

Fixes annual certificate budget as a share of GDP.

Permits Medicare and Medicaid to expire, and eliminates employer-based health insurance plan tax breaks.

6

National Environmental &
Energy Policy

*The world we have made, as a result of the level of thinking
we have done thus far, creates problems we cannot
solve at the same level of thinking at which we created them.*
Albert Einstein

NEVER HAS THERE BEEN a more critical time for instituting a comprehensive global environmental policy than by capitalizing on America's potential leadership role to focus upon the three seminal pillars of the present global environmental threat: global warming, fresh water scarcity, and loss of biodiversity.

Without addressing each of these interlinked pillars with a program that balances the causal relationships of their inextricable interdependence, we will continue to offer Band-Aid solutions to protecting our global village, and the outcome is inevitable: continued deterioration of quality of life, increased health crises, out-of-control energy costs, loss of arable land, poisoning of fresh and salt water resources, and military adventurism to seize and control fossil fuel resources.

The U.S. has not been "late" coming to the table to embrace the root causes of global warming; it has been "absent" in all substantive discussions relating to implementation of the Kyoto Protocol. At the federal level, we have totally abdicated our responsibility to protect the global environment.

As chairman of the Senate subcommittees on water resources, environmental pollution, and energy in the 1970s, I co-sponsored and in some cases co-authored every meaningful piece of legislation dealing with water, air, waste, pollution, and energy that was enacted into law.

We have pulled back from those advances and now, in the 21st Century, we are bent on literally destroying the resources we depend upon for life on our planet. Without swift and aggressive collective efforts by the entire global community to address these threats, the price future generations will pay will be catastrophic.

My environmental/energy policy will be a global policy, with the U.S. leading the world into a new and all-encompassing responsible environmental future.

GLOBAL WARMING—IN EFFECT, CLIMATE CHANGE— is at the crux of the environmental crisis forced by the accelerating use of fossil fuels and carbon-induced climate change. We Americans are disproportionate contributors to this phenomenon. We represent just 5% of the world's population, but consume more than 30% of the world's nonrenewable carbon resources (petroleum, coal and natural gas). However, the rest of the world is catching up in this deadly race; China will soon surpass the U.S., and India is rapidly closing the gap as major carbon emitters.

Bold initiatives, going beyond Kyoto, are called for if this trend is to be reversed. Negotiations have already begun to address the post-2012 era, when the Kyoto guidelines expire. The U.S. must take the lead in the next round. I propose that a Global Carbon Cap (GCC) be created as part of the post-Kyoto Protocol of the United Nations Framework Convention on Climate Change. This GCC would go beyond greenhouse gas emissions reduction and be based on reduction in the use of fossil fuels. In addition to capping carbon emissions, a Global Carbon Tax would be instituted.

The Carbon Tax would fund an International Consortium to bring together the global scientific and engineering communities to cooperatively develop technologies that could get the world off carbon-based fuel dependency in a decade.

Conventional crude oil supplies won't keep up with growing global demand in the next 25 years. Other fuels from ethanol to liquefied coal and oil from tar sands will be tapped to close the gap, says a National Petroleum Industry report—all of which diminish fresh water supplies. This is a scenario for planetary disaster. Further, worldwide energy use is projected to double by 2040 and triple by 2070.

The International Energy Agency and the U.S. Energy Information Administration project total liquid fuel production of 116 million to 118 million barrels a day by 2030. International oil companies indicated that amount may not be achievable. Today, global crude oil production is about 85 million barrels a day, barely 70% of the projected demand in 25 years.

The nation's electricity grid is a more immediate problem. Since 1990, the U.S. has experienced a 30% shortfall in electrical capacity. It is predicted that by 2012, the U.S. will experience "rolling blackouts" as a result of the shortage of natural gas and an over-capacity and badly outdated electricity grid.

Even if the U.S. and the world could meet the energy demands of the future through increased fossil fuel production, the environmental downside is that we would live in a world only marginally fit for human habitation, since the increase in carbon dioxide emissions would increase from six billion tons in 2000 to an estimated 20 billion tons by 2100.

Lobbyist-induced conventional wisdom suggests that ethanol and other bio-fuels are the panacea to our energy crisis. This is simply faulty logic. Consider the National Academy of Sciences' statement that even if all of the corn in the U.S. were used for ethanol production, it would only displace 12% of the gasoline now used. Moreover, corn ethanol is not sustainable because growing corn erodes the soil 18 times faster than it can recover, and ethanol typically requires more fossil fuels to make it from corn than it provides as fuel. Finally, and perhaps most importantly, while it takes 18 gallons of water to make a gallon of gasoline from crude oil, it takes over **12,000 gallons of water to make an equivalent gallon of ethanol** from corn! The Organization for Economic Co-operation and Development (OECD) study has concluded, "...the overall environmental impacts of ethanol and bio-diesel can very easily exceed those of petrol and mineral diesel."

The final nail in the ethanol coffin is driven in by FarmEcon.com: "Ethanol is not a cheap source of energy; it is about three times as expensive as gasoline."

So where does this leave us? Our options are crystal clear: move from carbon dependency to renewable and alternative energy sources, or under the best scenario, risk living on a planet without the quality of life we enjoy today. And under the worse scenario, cook the human race off the planet within a century. These changes will be difficult, costly, politically challenging, and technologically demanding, but completely within the character of the creativity of the human spirit, and ultimately economically sound.

BIODIVERSITY IS AN UNDER-APPRECIATED LOSS. Over the centuries, man's intellect has fueled a growth in population, industrialization, and technological advancement that has outstripped the earth's ability to keep pace. As Bo Ekman, founder of the Swedish Tällberg Foundation, established to further the understanding of change patterns in the world, recently said, "...human life needs food ...water, energy and air. ...Human beings need the earth, but earth does not actually need us."

Rising sea levels will have severe impacts in low-lying coastal communities throughout the world. Melting of the polar ice cap could raise sea levels by 20 feet or more—a level that would permanently flood virtually all major coastal cities.

WITHOUT WATER, there is no life, making the availability of fresh water worldwide the greatest challenge facing us—even greater than global warming. Already one-sixth of the earth's population—over one billion people—doesn't have access to adequate fresh water.

Global warming is the cause of much of the loss of fresh water around the world. The melting of mountain glaciers threatens water supplies of cities and entire countries from the U.S. to Asia. Nobel Prize winner in chemistry Mario Molina warned that climate change and inappropriate water management might intensify global warming by the end of this century, creating "an intolerable risk."

Already rains and droughts are related to climate change and to the melting of glaciers. Climate change has exacerbated flooding and water scarcity. Climate change is having a significant effect on global weather patterns, causing both more floods and more droughts, and again the loss of fresh water. It has the potential of inflicting damage on all of the major ecosystems on the planet, thereby threatening the biodiversity of these ecosystems—and therefore life itself.

The world is a awash with outstanding conservation organizations, NGOs, and potentially effective industry programs such as the Marine Stewardship Council and the Forest Stewardship Council to ensure protection of scarce biological resources. These efforts should remain at the forefront of our nation's biodiversity protection policy.

The greatest threat to biodiversity is global warming. Succeed in capping carbon emissions, and the rest of the environmental threats become manageable. Fail and best efforts of well-meaning organizations are nothing more than Band-Aid solutions.

THERE ARE COST EFFECTIVE SOLUTIONS. As somber as the above assessment of the current global environmental crisis is, we are not without options. Through a thoughtful, concerted commitment to energy efficiency and the development of alternative energy resources, we can maintain a strong industrial base while ensuring a livable planet for our children—one on which they will enjoy clean air, abundant fresh water, and unpolluted ecosystems.

Many have attempted to isolate energy policy from environmental policy. This is simply not possible. All energy sources have their basis in the environment, whether the source is coal, oil, gas, nuclear, agricultural, wind, solar or geothermal. And during the conversion of the energy source into commercial energy, there is a direct impact on the environment: air quality, water quality, and global warming. Finally, there is the impact of the disposal of the spent fuel—land, air and water all are directly or indirectly adversely affected. In addition to energy-generated waste, solid waste disposal is threatening ground water throughout the United States.

Therefore, while I have drafted a detailed energy program, my environmental policy necessarily includes energy use as the cornerstone.

To be effective, a comprehensive environmental policy must be global in concept and yet able to be implemented regionally and locally as conditions dictate.

My environmental policy builds upon three constructs: reducing CO_2 emissions, protecting and cleaning up fresh water resources, and protecting and enhancing ecosystems that are significant "carbon sinks" such as the world's forests and wetlands.

TRANSPORTATION AND POWER GENERATION together account for over 60% of carbon dioxide emissions in the U.S. Therefore, focusing on reducing these non-point sources of CO_2 will have an immediate and positive impact on global warming. Tackling transportation-related CO_2 generation regularly raises the temperature of the global warming debate, since reducing the impact is often associated with life-style changes: smaller, more fuel-efficient cars, use of mass transit, alternative fuels, and car pooling.

Yes, these are viable options and part of the total solution; and any complete CO_2 reduction program will necessarily include these elements. But, with technological advances promoted by the R & D funding from a Global Carbon Tax, the impact of these solutions does not have to be life-changing.

An immediate focus to increase efficiency in personal vehicles will be through enactment of tough CAFE standards, at a minimum matching the European-Euro VI emission levels, and pressing forward for intensified development of hybrid technology. A crash program to commercialize hydrogen-fueled vehicles will be enacted to make this the intercity personal vehicle choice. Hydrogen-powered vehicles are already on the streets of Las Vegas and a number of other cities; Norway has a 360-mile intercity highway with hydrogen refueling stations. And North Dakota has commissioned its first wind-to-hydrogen facility.

With the greatly enhanced storage capacity of new-generation batteries and the rapidly declining cost of fuel cells, fuel cell and electric-powered personal carriers will become the intra-city and commuters' vehicle of choice.

The U.S. has a rail network of over 100,000 miles, and yet as one crusty railroad president once said, "If you have to heat it, cool it, feed it, water it or relieve it, we don't haul it," to which the interlocutor asked, "What do you haul?" The answer: "Coal, boy, coal." And, so it has been since the advent of the interstate highway system. Freight in the U.S. has by and large abandoned the rails, and the cost in terms of CO_2 emissions and global warming has been enormous.

Funding the upgrading and expansion of the U.S. rail system to unload our highways, cities and ports by providing greatly increased piggyback transport for freight can significantly decrease carbon emissions. We need a national policy to electrify and upgrade the entire existing trunk rail system to provide a fast, low-carbon freight network for the U.S., thus unloading overcrowded interstate highways.

High-speed interstate passenger transportation will be modernized through development of a National Interstate Magnetic Levitation Rail System (maglev), built by sharing the Interstate Highway system's right of way. Maglev is a proven technology already operating in China, which operates trains at speeds of over 300 mph.

With new generation trains and maglev technology, passenger services between East coast cities, and between certain high-traffic Western cities, can be made faster, safer, cheaper, and less carbon intensive than driving. And, emerging technologies for "personal high-speed" people-movers using fixed guide-way systems similar to monorails will provide an intra-city transportation system, greatly reducing the need for personal vehicles, taxis, and on-the-road transportation systems, thus cleaning-up, speeding-up, and decongesting our metropolitan areas.

These rail revolutions will re-channel and employ the resources of the military industrial complex, which will have spare capacity as a result of our ending the Iraq War and avoiding future unnecessary military adventures. Of course, that's after reordering our national priorities toward a rational defense posture. Focusing our country's technological R & D capabilities on solving the transportation gridlock of our cities, and expediting the interstate movement of freight and passengers will rank alongside the computer revolution as the second greatest technical advance of this century, unleashing the full capability of human productivity—presently gridlocked.

FOSSIL FUEL POWER PLANTS rarely achieve conversion efficiency greater than 40%, and transmission losses on the U.S. power grid are estimated at 7-9%, so nearly one-half of all fossil fuel energy is lost before being put to any productive use.

Air pollution is an increasingly serious problem, with electricity generation a major contributor. A recent Department of Defense report cited by respected scientist Amory Lovins states, "Studies show that oil pollution causes at least $4.6 billion in damages each year to crops, forests, rivers." Research indicates one pollutant, fine particulates, may be responsible for 64,000 deaths each year—more than the number of people killed in automobile accidents. Other fossil fuel based pollutants include sulfur dioxide and nitrogen oxides. It is time for a more efficient and environmentally sound scenario.

In 1978, as the chairman of the Senate Energy subcommittee I saw to the enactment of the Energy Act of 1978 (PURPA). This bill sought to decrease the nation's dependence on foreign oil and increase domestic energy conservation and efficiency. PURPA promoted development of facilities to generate electricity from renewable energy sources and required that power stations purchase excess generated electricity at voided cost. That incentive included for small hydro is still in place today to encourage incentives for purchasing excesses of wind and solar energy.

One-third of the new electricity generated worldwide already comes from renewable sources. Just a few years ago, hydroelectric and limited geothermal were the mainstays of renewable energy. Now, through technological advances, wind, solar, tidal and hydrogen power are becoming economically viable and technically possible.

The panoply of alternative and renewable energy options continues to grow rapidly. Wind and solar are the most obvious choices for rapid assimilation into the energy production matrix. The shortcomings of both of these sources have been their unpredictability and/or lack of consistency. But, with an improved distribution grid, solar, solar thermal, and wind can be directly connected to the national grid.

Solar and wind can also be used as power sources for production of electricity for other alternative energy sources. Solar is currently being used to recharge batteries in many applications worldwide. Scaling up these applications to commercial size is presently under development.

Wind power and solar power are both already being used for the production of hydrogen fuel. As this becomes commercially viable, hydrogen with its only byproduct water promises to virtually eliminate the need for fossil fuel in personal as well as mass transportation. The work of Justin Sutton bringing the technology of hydrogen-powered maglev with solar panels encasing conduits to transport liquid hydrogen and electric grid power creating a hydrogen super highway is at the demonstration stage.

A high-capacity superconducting energy pipeline, or SuperGrid, could deliver electricity and hydrogen fuel across the nation and help meet future energy needs while reducing the consumption of fossil fuels, say experts who recently assessed the scientific feasibility of the idea. The SuperGrid is a liquid hydrogen pipeline with the high-tension electric lines carried within the pipeline and cooled by the liquid hydrogen. The idea of a continental SuperGrid has been proposed by Chauncey Starr, founder and president emeritus of the Electric Power Research Institute. "We found no showstoppers to the proposed SuperGrid concept," said Thomas Overbye, a professor of electrical and computer engineering at *University of Illinois at Urbana-Champaign*. "By delivering both electrical power and hydrogen fuel, the SuperGrid could help eliminate transmission bottlenecks, improve system reliability and meet growing energy demands well into the 21st Century."

Of course many experts still see nuclear energy as the panacea of power generation, but the serious issues of safety and waste disposal continue to cast shadows on this technology. In the Senate, I opposed the government's nuclear fission policy in the 1970s, successfully limiting it to those plants on the drawing boards. However, the nuclear fusion option should be kept open. The Chinese Tokamak fusion device is nearing test status and deserves close attention. Should it prove viable, the U.S. should jointly fund commercialization of nuclear fusion power generation along with other nations through the global carbon tax pool.

The U.S. must take a strong stand to combat global warming. The front-line defense must be legislation, which reduces carbon emissions across the board. This legislation must reduce carbon at every point of emissions, not merely at the primary producer level, i.e., coal-fired power plants and oil refineries. It must also go straight to the sources of local impact, i.e. auto emissions, and local industry.

Fear mongers have tried to instill in the public a belief that taking effective, strong action to reduce carbon emissions will put American industry in peril by rendering it non-competitive against foreign manufacturers. There is a very simple and effective method of insuring that U.S. competitiveness is not harmed, and in fact, due to our proven technological superiority, it would be enhanced.

The World Trade Organization (WTO) has no specific agreement dealing with the environment. However, the WTO agreements confirm governments' right to protect the environment. The objectives of sustainable development and environmental protection are certainly within the gambit of the WTO. Therefore, enacting strong legislation in the U.S., tying foreign trade to U.S. emissions standards, would be appropriate within the constructs of the WTO. And, if not, then the WTO charter could be amended accordingly.

Carbon Reduction Legislation will include a provision that any country importing into the U.S. must enact and enforce emissions standards equal to or greater than those in the U.S. This legislation, at the country level, must be enacted on an industry-specific basis for all industries producing goods or services destined for the U.S.

The impact of this legislation will be two-fold. First, it will ensure that there is no further diminishing of U.S. competitiveness on an industry-by-industry basis, and may increase U.S. competitiveness since the U.S. already has some environmental standards in place. And secondly, U.S. technology developed to reduce carbon emissions will become a major export of the U.S. to countries wishing to do business with the U.S.

This proposal will ensure that global warming will be attacked head-on, and that U.S. leadership will be worldwide in reducing carbon emissions. The perceived loopholes and reduction of U.S. competitiveness will be eliminated and, in fact, turned into a major U.S. competitive advantage while exhibiting environmental leadership.

SPACE REPRESENTS A LIMITLESS FRONTIER for humankind. Laws modeled on the Law of the Sea need to be agreed upon to make energy, natural resources, and knowledge available in a manner that fosters greater cooperation, rather than greater competition, among all nations. In keeping with this spirit, space must not be militarized.

Recent developments suggest that space-based solar power is a feasible technology to deliver electrical energy to the earth at costs competitive with coal and nuclear, but with virtually no carbon emissions other than those involved in the construction of the initial infrastructure. Concurrently, highly promising technologies are emerging to significantly lower launch costs, creating the opportunity for space-related industrial development with hundreds of thousands of well-paid jobs.

The U.S. has been the leader in space-related development from the time of President John Kennedy. It is time to exercise space leadership again. I call on the U.S. to lead a global space development effort to deploy working space-based solar energy systems by 2020 that deliver significant power to user nations and that provide for the following:

- ✓ Low-cost launch, including consideration of space elevators and other advanced technology.

- ✓ Use of lunar and other non-terrestrial resources. Our moon has abundant supplies of most materials required to construct facilities and human habitats in space.

- ✓ Delivery of power at competitive costs, including to the currently poorly served in developing countries.

IN CONCLUDING, one may reflect upon the preceding paragraphs and wonder if I have articulated an energy policy or an environmental policy. The answer is the two are inextricably intertwined. Such has not always been the case. Nature could renew her resources faster than man could exploit them, prior to industrialization. But with the advent of the atomic era, man has shown and is now proving that he can thwart the best efforts of nature to ensure the livability of our planet. There is no ecosystem that is safe from our exploitation and despoliation. If we cannot touch them directly, we certainly disrupt them through our waste disposal on land and in the sea.

Perhaps Jeremy Rifkin, president of the Foundation on Economic Trends, states it most presciently:

> The looming peak in global production of conventional crude oil is being played out against the backdrop of two other potentially destabilizing forces: the rise of Islamic fundamentalism in the Middle East and around the world and increased warming of the Earth's climate from the burning of fossil fuels. The synergistic effects of each of these phenomena on the others will be critical in determining the prospects for human civilization in the coming century.

The Congress, held hostage by energy-related special interests, may find it impossible to act in a timely way on the environmental threat. If the American voters are empowered as lawmakers, they certainly would establish a carbon tax and aggressively pursue much of the above programs. After all, they are the ones to suffer the consequences.

An Environmental/Energy Policy

1. Environmental policy based upon:
   a. Reducing greenhouse gases and CO_2 emissions.
   b. Protecting and rejuvenating fresh water resources.
   c. Protecting and enhancing ecosystems that are significant "carbon sinks."

2. Cap global warming with a Global Carbon Tax used to fund international R & D to develop commercially-viable renewable energy technologies.

3. Transportation CO_2 reduction:
   a. Euro IV-CAFE standards and increased hybridization.
   b. Crash program for hydrogen-powered vehicles.
   c. Mass transit-high speed intercity rail (maglev)
   d. Electrification of rail trunk lines for freight.

4. Power generation:
   a. Create a SuperGrid to distribute hydrogen and electricity.
   b. Develop carbon-free space-based solar power generation capability and a space industrialization infrastructure.
   c. Connect solar, wind and geo-thermal generators to the grid.
   d. Explore nuclear *fusion* with China's Tokamak.

5. Protect the environment and U.S. industry's competitiveness through the implementation of regulations via the WTO.

7

The War on Drugs

*The income of the drug barons is greater
than the American defense budget.
With this financial power they can suborn
the institutions of the state,
and if the state resists they can purchase
the firepower to outgun it.*
Judge Gomez Hurtado
Colombian High Court
1993

FOR 12 GRUELING YEARS, New Jersey State Police Lt. Jack Cole was an undercover agent on the front lines of the drug war. He's exactly the kind of cop you'd hope to find in a job like that—rock steady, fearless, and dependable as the sunrise. And he was successful—one of the best in the department.

But nearing retirement in 2003 he looked back over the thousands of hours of danger and deception and decided that maybe he had not really accomplished anything. In fact he might have made things worse.

Here was an honest cop who had lost faith in his mission. So he changed missions. Now Lt. Cole is trying to end the drug war. Three years ago, he and several of his fellow officers founded LEAP—Law Enforcement Against Prohibition—and already some 500 other law enforcement officers, judges, and prosecutors have joined them.

Drug prohibition, like alcohol prohibition, actually got started back in the 1920s, but most of us think of President Nixon as the man who started the War on Drugs. Nixon took the Bureau of Narcotics, a tiny federal agency with a few hundred employees, and turned it into the DEA, a vast international police force with more power then than the FBI and CIA combined. And it was Nixon who got Congress to open the public coffers to local law enforcement.

All of a sudden federal money began raining down on police departments all over the country, and Jack Cole was there when it happened. "We had a seven-man narcotics unit," he says. "It always seemed perfectly adequate for the job we had to do. Then overnight we went from a seven-man unit to a 76-man narcotics bureau."

So now they had to justify this additional funding, and that called for a dramatic increase in drug busts. "They took undercover people like myself," says Cole, "and they targeted us against small friendship groups—groups of young people in college. And as soon as we got in there and became their friends, come Friday night, somebody'd say, 'Hey, school's out, we're off work, anyone want to get high?' And of course, if nobody said that, it was our job to say it." For a young officer on the way up it was a great game and he was good at it. "If somebody simply passed a marijuana cigarette to me, they became a drug dealer. That one marijuana cigarette would send that person to jail for seven years." Today when he talks about that success his voice is almost a whisper. "Over a thousand young people went to jail as a direct result of what I did as one undercover agent...something I'm certainly not proud of today."

Lt. Cole came to understand what a lot of us already suspected: the Drug War was fatally flawed from the get-go. In fact, when we ended alcohol prohibition in 1933 we should have ended drug prohibition for all the same reasons: to stop the skyrocketing murder rates, the corruption at all levels, and a criminal underworld growing by leaps and bounds—all the while the booze and drugs continued to flow unabated.

The problem was—and is—not much of a constituency for treating drug addicts as human beings. The numbers clearly show that there never were—and are not now—enough narcotics users in this country to raise concern. When the first drug laws were passed in 1914 we had maybe 300,000 addicts in the whole U.S.—less than half of 1% of the population. Today, after spending a trillion dollars and filling our vast and growing prison complex to the max, we have driven the rate of addiction *up*—not down—to nearly 2%. That's a 500% increase, but we're still talking about a very small slice of the population. But for some reason we have focused our most threatening legal artillery on this group. Instead of giving them treatment—proven to be many times cheaper and many times more effective than incarceration—we'd rather send them off to prison where they can often get all the drugs they want.

If you include all costs—interdiction, including use of the military, police, courts, and prisons—we're spending around $70 billion a year on this insane enterprise; and as Lt. Cole says, we're making the problem worse day by day. And this is not only here in the U.S. Our War on Drugs has also been a war on the countries that grow poppies and marijuana which have become the havens for crime and corruption. The whole point of prohibition is to make some prohibitive substances "prohibitively" expensive. Unfortunately, it becomes extremely attractive to organized crime.

Prohibition didn't work with alcohol and it's not working with drugs. Today both heroin and cocaine are cheaper, purer, and more available than ever before. Even worse, we've created a whole new generation of Al Capones with enough cash, influence, and firepower to threaten the country's foundations.

So what do we do?

We get the profit out of the illegal drug market.

In 1933, we did not end alcohol Prohibition because we suddenly decided alcohol wasn't dangerous. It's plenty dangerous. We ended Prohibition because the crime and violence was out of control *and we were getting nowhere*. That sounds like a pretty fair description of where we are in the drug war.

Immediately after Prohibition was repealed, the U.S. murder rate began to drop precipitously; and over the next decade it was down by half—a stunning success. Of course, we still had an alcohol problem but now we could try to get the victims into AA instead of having shoot-outs with their suppliers. Alcohol distribution today—tightly regulated and heavily taxed—clearly does a better job of keeping booze away from the kids than when the Mob was running the show. You never hear about whiskey pushers hanging around the schoolyard. There's no money in it.

And that's the key to the whole drug problem: get the money out of the equation. The best way to keep hard drugs like heroin and cocaine away from kids is to make the market financially unrewarding to criminals. Organized crime can't make a living on teenagers, amateurs and tourists. They need the daily hard core addicts, the one or two people out of a hundred who have to have the stuff right now. If we could take this small segment of the population out of the market, there would be no market. For 90 years, we have tried to get these folks to give up their drug habits by using threats and intimidation. We have had a notorious lack of success.

Maybe we ought to consider another approach. The Swiss, for example, stepped outside the prohibition box and came up with a completely original plan for dealing with chronic heroin addicts. They found 1,000 "incorrigibles"—people who had been through rehab more than once—and just gave them the drugs. The results were astonishing. Once the subjects were stabilized on a dependable dose of heroin, they didn't nod out—they *went* out—and got jobs. Half the unemployed found work, crime dropped by 60%, the homeless found housing, and general health improved all around.

And there was another amazing footnote to this experiment. Eighty-three of these hard-core users decided, on their own, to give up drugs. It seems that when uncertainty, fear and desperation are replaced by dependable government drug supplies, people are able to think more clearly and can sometimes decide to straighten out their lives. This voluntary abstinence ratio—8.3%—is a better cure rate than we get from most of our forced treatment programs. There are experiments like this going on all around the world as more and more countries turn away from the draconian drug prohibition the U.S. has championed for the last century. When the Dutch decriminalized the sale of marijuana in 1978 there were cries of outrage and alarm from Washington. Today, teenage marijuana use in Holland is *half* that of the U.S. As one Dutch official put it, "We have succeeded in making pot boring."

Where do we go from here?

The first thing we have to do is change the official classification of marijuana so sick people, at least, can have immediate access to it. Right now, the federal government still claims that marijuana has no medical value. That position is absurd, and it flies in the face of overwhelming scientific evidence. The value of marijuana as medicine is now solidly established in the medical literature here and abroad. The latest research indicates that the THC in marijuana shrinks cancer tumors. Let me say that again: The latest research indicates that the THC in marijuana shrinks cancer tumors.

Washington may be asleep at the switch, but the American people have already made up their minds on this issue. In the latest national poll, 80% of the voters support access to marijuana with a doctor's recommendation. Twelve states have already adopted legislation to make this happen.

Marijuana has been a political football since the 1960s, and it's time we stopped playing this silly and destructive game. We should assemble the leading medical and scientific experts and have them conduct an exhaustive study of every aspect of the marijuana problem and then we... Wait a minute. We already did that.

In 1972, Richard Nixon called for exactly that kind of study. He established the National Commission on Marihuana and Drug Abuse, and the so-called "Shafer Report" is regarded as the most thorough examination of the cannabis plant in history. It was endorsed by the AMA, the ABA, the American Association for Public Health, the NEA, and the National Council of Churches. Their recommendation? *Legalize marijuana.* Though this conclusion was the product of two years of research by some of the best minds available, it did not fit with the president's political agenda; and the report was deep-sixed. We should resurrect it.

As for the hard drugs, that's a much harder problem; but it should be clear by now that police, no matter how dedicated, are not going to be able to fix it. Law enforcement is much too blunt an instrument.

If you're trying to turn a screw, you only make things worse with a hammer. Before 1914, there were no drug criminals or drug crimes in the United States. If you were addicted to heroin in those days you went to the doctor, who wrote a prescription, and you took it to the drug store. As astounding as it sounds to us, most of these addicts lived otherwise productive lives. The drugs simply allowed them to function and as long as the dose was correct, the side effects were minimal. The vast majority of narcotics addicts at the time were paying their taxes and holding down jobs. Like diabetics, they had a medical problem that they worked out with their doctors.

It will be tough to turn this juggernaut around. There are tens of thousands of politicians, bureaucrats, police officers, prison guards and attorneys who receive most or all of their paycheck from this failed campaign. Even though they know the ship is dead in the water, they're not about to jump overboard.

Drug usage is a public health problem, not a criminal problem. It's the War on Drugs—the war against the criminal element—that ravages our inner cities and compounds the social damage of an errant social policy.

As in 1933, once we've got the money and the guns off the table, we can concentrate on our addiction problem. It won't be easy, but at least we won't have to pour money down a rat hole by arresting a million otherwise innocent people every year.

But for all the failures, we have had one outstanding success in the War on Drugs, a stunning victory that calls for our attention because it clearly shows a way out. Over the last 15 years, adult use of tobacco in the U.S. has dropped by 50%. The secret weapon? Education.

We never fired a shot.

We need to throw a lifeline to those of us addicted to drugs. We are all addicts to some degree—such is the advance of pharmacology. However, advanced drug addiction is a public health, not a criminal problem. There is a tremendous amount of human and technological talent tied up in the DEA and other agencies involved in the drug war. Imagine taking these powerful assets—complete with a global intelligence network—and focusing it on tracking terrorists.

It is difficult to appreciate the damage we do to other nations and their people when we focus our foreign aid on military and police equipment to permit autocratic regimes to better maintain themselves in power. We would be well advised to revisit some of our agricultural tariff policies as an effective way to wean foreign farmers from a dependency on narcotic cultivation.

The Drug War

Treats drug addiction as a criminal problem rather than a public health problem.

Ravages our inner cities and destroys family cohesion.

Militarizes our foreign policy, destabilizes democratic regimes and strengthens autocratic regimes.

Produces a prison system that incarcerates more people than any other country.

Fails to accept the presidential Shafer Commission recommendations to decriminalize drugs and treat addiction as a public health problem.

Is a de facto race and economic war.

8

Crime & Punishment

As long as we permit unfair laws to exist,
deny speedy trials or equal justice to all, and
operate prisons to punish rather than to rehabilitate,
our society will be guilty of a far greater crime
than any committed by those it prosecutes.
Anonymous

AS FAR BACK AS 1760 BC, the Code of Hammurabi provided the first organized set of laws to make people accountable for violations against others. The comprehensive laws governed virtually every aspect of human conduct, from contracts to property rights, from marriage to medical malpractice, and from crime to compensation. While the punishment for certain crimes, which we would deem misdemeanors today, was extreme, the laws gave citizens a code of conduct by which they could measure their daily activities.

Since then, nations and their governments have faced the choice of one of two fundamental risks. One is to seek total control of the lives of their citizens, so as to ensure "order" and "security," but at the risk of a bloody and destructive revolution when the collective human spirit can no longer abide such repression.

The other is to risk the broadest possible freedom for all citizens in the belief that people in a democratic society will so flourish in such freedom that their national common sense will ultimately repel the periodic tides of demagoguery or anarchy, which flow in and out of their lives.

The founding fathers of the United States chose to take the risk that comes with freedom, and they embodied it in that remarkable document known as the Bill of Rights. Unfortunately, a repressive climate engendered by fear has enveloped this country since the Second World War, which has severely threatened the fundamental protections the Bill of Rights affords all Americans.

Many factors have contributed to the current climate of repression; they began long before the Bush Administration took office. Most factors are rather obvious: our huge and rapidly growing and highly diverse population; our urban sprawl; our fast-paced, high-tech communications; our economic interdependence; and our gigantic government bureaucracy; our greedy corporate elites; our racial tensions—slavery's legacy; biblically-based homophobic fears; making scapegoats of immigrants to hide from national failings; changes in the definition of family; and the increasing disparity between the rich and poor.

Our lifestyle changes have accelerated at unprecedented speed, as the world has shrunk through globalization and information technology explodes with the World Wide Web (Internet). Instantly, we are made aware, in glaring detail, of starvation in Sudan, tsunamis in Indonesia, levee breaches in New Orleans, and wars in Iraq and Afghanistan.

Rising awareness has also exposed corporate corruption, chronic hunger and illiteracy, torture in our nation's prisons, the plight of the poverty-stricken in our inner cities, and the inequalities of race, gender, and sexual orientation. We have confronted discrimination at every level of society, yet we remain a society in which injustice prevails and, sadly, continues to grow.

We have witnessed worldwide protests against war, the death penalty, hunger, and inequality. Instead of responding positively to these cries for social change and justice, the entrenched powers have sought to control the ideas that threaten their own agendas of domination. If that meant violating longstanding rights, so be it. Most often, these violations have been cloaked in secrecy.

As pressure for societal change; e.g. equal rights, increased, those seeking to halt the change sought more control. The agents of repression rather than seek control over and changing the conditions creating the pressures addressed the comfortable, settled, generally contented and traditional middle and upper class instilling fear in them of menacing stereotypes of crime, drugs, and permissiveness.

THE REPRESSION OF COMMUNICATIONS, the avenues through which people sharpen their awareness and publicize their new demands that upset the status quo, is the traditional course taken to circumscribe freedom. In the history of our great nation, there never has been an administration that so deliberately sought to undermine and control the dissemination of information to the public, to restrict free expression of opinion, and to criminalize dissent as the present one.

The rights of speech, peaceable assembly, dissent, freedom of the press, due process, privacy, the practice of one's religion, and the right to bear arms—all guaranteed by the Bill of Rights and amendments to the United States Constitution—have never been closer to annihilation.

In the midst of social turmoil, we have "dumbed down" America, left all children behind, outsourced vast amounts of work, privatized customary government tasks, misappropriated funds for the upkeep of our nation's infrastructure, and funneled billions of taxpayer dollars for war at the expense of the social needs of our people.

"When hope dies, its heirs are desperation and despair," said the great educator Dr. James B. Conant. Today that prophecy has come true. Hope has indeed died for vast numbers of Americans, and desperation has become embodied in the social dynamite we call "street crime."

As a backdrop of these developing conditions, America has slid into a criminal justice quagmire that, in a matter of 35 years, has given us the highest incarceration rate of any nation on earth. A poster announces: THAT ONE IN 133 AMERICANS IS INCARCERATED IS NOT A NATIONAL STATISTIC. IT IS A NATIONAL TRAGEDY. I would add a *shameful* tragedy.

Today, the least infraction is punishable by fines, jail time or worse: political and social protests, possession of marijuana, and even wearing a t-shirt that criticizes the president. Crime statistics are down, but incarceration rates continue to climb. To put that problem into perspective, before Presidents Nixon, Reagan, and the first Bush made a serious case for the War on Drugs, only 315,000 men and women were incarcerated in state and federal prisons. That number tripled by the time Clinton became president and has continued to climb.

According to the Sentencing Project, criminologists Alfred Blumstein and Allen Beck concluded that changes in crime explain only 12% of the prison rise, while changes in sentencing policy account for 88% of the increase. Let's look at sentencing policy and how it has led us into this dismal state of affairs we now face in our criminal justice system.

POLITICAL LEADERSHIP—PRIMARILY REPUBLICAN—HAS BEQUEATHED THE U.S. A MISGUIDED SENTENCING POLICY. In 1920, prohibition of alcohol, then America's most popular recreational drug, commenced with crackdowns across the country. Prohibition was an abysmal failure. It opened wide the doors to bootleg liquor, organized crime, and lucrative ventures for those who dared participate in the illegal trade of alcohol. Above all, it bred disrespect for the law. In 1933, alcohol prohibition laws were repealed, largely due to public pressure and a courageous leader—Franklin Roosevelt.

In the previous chapter, we tackled the War on Drugs and its abject failure. You would think we would have learned from Prohibition that criminalizing drug use does not work. The revised War on Drugs, so dubbed by Richard Nixon in 1972, spawned a flood of get-tough laws at the local, state, and federal levels of government and launched a tidal wave of money-making opportunities for those involved in policing, prosecuting, and punishing violators at every level in both the public and private sectors.

As Milton Friedman, the late Nobel Prize winning economist, said, "…if you look at the drug war from a purely economic point of view, the role of the government is to protect the drug cartel. That's literally true."

In 1973, under the direction of Governor Nelson Rockefeller (whose name evokes *moderate* Republicanism), New York introduced mandatory minimum sentences of 15 years to life imprisonment for the possession of more than four ounces of a hard drug. Along with many other governors, Michigan's Governor William G. Milliken answered the call to check the rising tide of drug trafficking in his state and signed the mandatory minimum law. He now denounces his decision. "We were trying to catch the kingpins, but instead we got a lot of little guys, some of whom were addicts trying to supply their habit. We did not foresee the problems that these laws would create."

The "three strikes and you're out" policy, first adopted in 1994 in California, became the first mandatory sentencing policy to gain widespread support and be adopted by most states. This policy mandates life imprisonment for a third criminal conviction for any offense. Carried to its extreme in the case of a young man arrested three times for stealing food and sentenced to life imprisonment, that case was overturned and, in the process, focused public attention on rethinking the problems with this particular get-tough policy.

Other problems of considerable weight and cost have resulted from mandatory sentencing, not the least of which has been stripping our judges of their discretionary powers. Prior to the new sentencing laws, judges used their powers to assess a given case and impose an appropriate sentence, so that the punishment most often fit the crime. With mandatory minimums, however, judges could not use their discretion, and instead handed down sentences far outweighing the crimes in most cases.

Quick to get on the "get tough" bandwagon were ambitious prosecutors and politicians, whose careers flourished by crackdowns on crime and drug dealing. In fact, the prison population grew so quickly that overcrowding resulted, mandating the construction of new state and federal prisons and the addition of corrections officers and management staff to handle the growing prison population. Overcrowding our prisons has brought additional problems: increased violence and higher risk of spreading diseases.

One of the most serious problems that resulted from the institution of the mandatory minimum laws has been the incarceration of non-violent offenders; more than half of today's prisoners are incarcerated on drug charges, despite evidence that treatment programs are more effective in preventing repeat offenses. The taxpayer dollars wasted on incarcerating non-violent offenders are incalculable. This is a shameful waste of the public treasure.

Our national sentencing policy has failed miserably. As Senior Circuit Judge Myron H. Bright of the 8th Circuit Court in 1993 so aptly said, "Unwise sentencing policies, which put men and women in prison for years, not only ruin lives, but also drain the American taxpayers. It is time to call a halt to the unnecessary and expensive cost of putting people in prison for a long time based on the mistaken notion that such an effort will win the War on Drugs. The public needs to know that unnecessary, harsh and unreasonable drug sentences serve to waste billions of dollars without doing much good for society. We have an unreasonable system."

THE NEGATIVE CULTURE of incarceration is our own creation. When people become acclimated to prison culture, they learn how to function better in that environment than they do in normal society. It would take a radical shift for them to change. Keeping the criminal justice system entrenched in that negative culture has been the work of three elements—economics, politics, and the media.

The answer is not in spending more money on programs but in changing the culture of incarceration. That requires a paradigm shift. This is about not having forced idleness over extended periods of time in our prisons, one of the worst situations you can impose on human beings. "We confine people to cages and treat them like they are incompetent, incapable, and unworthy, and we believe our job is to make their lives miserable," says Morgan Moss, director of the Center for Therapeutic Justice in Virginia. "That's the culture of negative environment, which is the prison system we now have. We forget that people go to prison *as* punishment not *for* punishment."

The most dangerous criminals represent only about 10% of the prison population nationwide, yet we're treating the other 90% the way the violent 10% are treated. Such treatment of drug addicts and alcoholics perpetuates the revolving door of recidivism by improving their criminal skills while in prison to better criminally finance the cost of their addictions when released. Until they receive proper treatment to check their addictions, they are going to remain caught in those revolving doors.

WE MUST CHANGE negative prison culture into positive opportunity. We must turn this negative culture into a positive environment, and we can start simply by treating prisoners with dignity and respect, as capable people. When you do so, remarkable things happen. They stop acting like caged animals. They no longer destroy property or endanger others. The suicide attempt rate plummets, and the violence across the board in prisons goes to almost zero.

"This works beyond a shadow of a doubt," attests Moss, who has practiced this method successfully in jails and believes it would work just as effectively in prisons. "When there is no forced idleness, because inmates are busy in volunteer, self-selected programs for 12 hours a day, the security staff has very little to do.

"When you treat prisoners as human beings deserving of dignity and respect, people change. The only ones that do not change are so damaged, so institutionalized, so mentally ill or so anti-social, they are incapable of changing." That is a different problem than what I am attempting to focus on in this chapter.

Stop and think for a moment that more than 600,000 people are released annually from our prisons, and more than 12 million people pass through the nation's jails every year. They come back into society either angry for having been abused and treated unfairly while incarcerated or prepared to merge into our communities ready, willing and able to become productive citizens. Which one would you prefer to have as a new neighbor? We train attack dogs through selective punishment. Why do politicians believe that they can get better results by punishing people?

We need more innovation in the courts building on successes with drug, reentry, and other problem-solving, courts with effective probation and parole supervision that lock people up as a last resort and not with technical probation violations. While they are in prison, we need to make the environment conducive to learning and rehabilitating, helping inmates make the most of their time. When they are released, where there are functional families, support should be made available so that the families can better receive them and be educated in ways of keeping them on the track of productivity. To support the family's efforts, probation and parole must offer positive intervention. Often, however, there are no functional families; in those cases, mentoring needs to be encouraged by faith-based and other volunteer organizations. It is absolutely critical that basic needs such as housing, medical care, and work are available. A person who is denied basic needs is forced by society to operate in an extralegal environment to survive.

If this approach were taken across the country, within a decade, significant progress could be made in changing the culture of the American criminal justice system. Locking up people for $30,000 or more per year for lengthy sentences is extremely wasteful. Moreover, it is a human, social, and moral waste that can no longer be afforded nor tolerated. Other countries that do not spend such vast resources on creating negative human capital will knock our socks off competitively unless we make the decision to end this waste.

Forty years ago, Karl Menninger, M.D., in his book, *The Crime of Punishment*, pointed to the deep flaws in our "corrections" systems. Instead of taking measures to correct the flaws identified by Menninger, state and national leaders responded to demagogic populist calls, fueled by manufactured political claims, to get tough on crime. They have created a monster that threatens not only the nation's competitiveness but our personal security. We have concentrated a vast army of troubled people together with hardened criminals and potential terrorists. We are beginning to see the emerging threat of terrorist gangs, taught in our prisons, paid for by taxpayers at a cost per annum equal to a Harvard education. The greatest threat to our nation may lie within our own prisons.

Our corrections system must be transformed to produce people more able to become productive citizens than when they entered the system. Nationally, over two-thirds of people who get entangled in the criminal justice system re-offend and return to the system.

The solution is indicated by the results. People who, while in prison, complete their higher education or participate in any number of programs designed to teach a work ethic and other values that can be applied in the real world when the prisoner is released, have a 3% recidivism rate. Clearly, making people more capable produces the desired results. Incarceration, with some exceptions, should present educational opportunities to every inmate to the maximum of their aspirations. If that aspiration includes a college education, then we should create that opportunity, since we have already committed to pay this price by incarcerating that individual.

It is possible to reduce our jail and prison population, now at 747 per 100,000, to levels comparable to Canada (129 per 100,000). Canada has a similarly diverse population with comparable levels of affluence and poverty. Since there are countries, such as Finland, that employ "gentle justice" and incarcerate far fewer people than Canada, we must look beyond our shores to those examples and elevate our long-term goals.

The guiding philosophy for change must be that the purpose of the criminal justice system is to assure public safety through changing the behavior of people who commit criminal acts and by giving offenders the opportunity to become more capable of leading productive lives in the open community through education and treatment of addictive behavior.

A strategy to implement this philosophy could reduce the American rate of incarceration to that comparable to Canada and other democracies within a decade. This would be a domestic Marshall Plan to:

- Revitalize poor, crime-ridden communities by presenting opportunities for economic, social, and political advancement.

- Change the paradigm of the corrections system as a whole from punishment to problem solving and rehabilitation.

- Replace enforced idleness in jails and prisons with intensive education, training, skill development, and substance abuse treatment.

- Eliminate or modify laws that create irrational barriers to employment for those with a criminal record.

- Create incentives to hire people with a criminal record, particularly those with non-violent drug-related offenses.

- Create opportunities for "boomer generation" retirees to get involved and apply their skills and experience through volunteering and mentorship to help people, their neighborhoods, and their communities to find their place in the "New America."

- Enact a federal law to give voting rights to felons who have paid their debt to society.

"Politics as usual" fosters irrational, counterproductive responses rather than effective solutions. Many political races are characterized by accusations that the other party is soft on crime. Talking tough on crime may win elections. But being tough on crime has worsened the problem by packing our prisons with non-violent offenders.

The only beneficiary of a tough-on-crime political posture is the prison-industrial complex. Its prime directive is more profit for its shareholders, who benefit by putting more and more people into the system. The rising costs of doing so are an unrecognized drain on our national competitiveness, especially the hidden cost of all the negative human capital created by the criminal justice system.

What must we do? We need leadership that does not flinch from the realities of the problem. We need a strategy for transformational change that can eliminate the threats to the country that have arisen due to misguided thinking in our criminal justice system. The recommendations in this chapter address the transformation that needs to take place in our criminal justice system for the survival of America as a nation of opportunity for people, regardless of their race or national origin.

The Problems

One of every 133 Americans was behind bars on June 30, 2006.

With only 5% of the world's population, the United States has over 25% of the world's incarcerated people.

The U.S. incarcerates the largest number of people in the world.

The U.S. imprisons the most women in the world.

As of 2004, the annual direct cost for incarceration exceeded $42 billion.

The Solutions

Create opportunities for direct citizen involvement through volunteer programs in prisons and jails, mentoring of released offenders, family outreach, and provision for citizen oversight boards for all levels of the criminal justice system.

Decriminalize the regulation of drugs.

Legalize marijuana, tax it, and make it available through regulated stores.

Eliminate mandatory minimum and three-strikes sentencing laws.

Treat drug addiction as the public health problem that it is.

Create alternatives to restrictive post-release correctional control for non-serious, non-violent offenders.

Offer release incentives to inmates for good behavior and education.

Treat the whole prisoner (economic, social, spiritual and physical).

Develop meaningful ways to strengthen families with incarcerated parents through regular, less restrictive visits in prison and much less costly telephone calls.

Offer parenting classes to inmates to help them better relate to their children and lend moral support to the caregiver of their children.

Work with children of inmates to boost self-esteem and understanding.

Support organizations that help offenders return to the community through training, housing, jobs, and reintegration programs.

Abolish the death penalty and become outraged at the waste of money, lives, and human potential in our criminal justice system.

9

Shrouded in Secrecy

Secrecy is the greatest threat to democracy.
It masks the accountability of government
officialdom. Absent the people with lawmaking
powers to correctively react to the revelations of
courageous whistleblowers, democratic society
will remain hostage to the culture of secrecy.
The tragedy is that little has changed in the last
30 years to alter the corruption of secrecy in
government and in the corporate sector. In fact,
it has gotten worse.
Mike Gravel

THE PREREQUISITE for a democracy is a responsible, enlightened citizenry. If the American people are ever to become meaningful participants in the operation of their government, there must be an end to national decision-making in secret and policy implementation by executive fiat. This requires easy access to virtually all information by the public and, with rare and precisely defined exceptions, the removal of all limits on the information available to its elected representatives. The government's shrill claims of a "need" for secrecy must give way to the higher priority of the citizen's need to be informed.

At present the scales are tipped heavily in favor of the government. Information is systematically classified and withheld from the public for vague reasons of "national security" and denied to Congress by the imperious assertion of "executive privilege." These tools of secrecy, when placed in knowing and manipulative hands, can be stretched and shaped far beyond what might be construed as legitimately sensitive defense and diplomatic data to provide self-appointed decision-makers with a protective shield against public accountability. It can be difficult, if not impossible, for even the most well-intentioned administrations to resist such "privilege" when the stakes involve executive prestige, personal vanity or political expediency.

As a result, American citizens know little more than what the state and its co-guardians of information in the mass media either want them to know or are permitted to let them know. Citizens often doubt the accuracy of what they are told, rightly suspect they are not being told everything, and resent the obvious lack of trust by the government in their ability to understand the issues and to make proper judgments even if provided with all the facts. They are inundated by propaganda communicated to them as gospel from far and wide in an endless stream of confusing and often conflicting images splashed across television screens or jumbled in newspaper headlines. There is, however, little citizens can know firsthand or with the certainty that they are not being lied to; conned by the complex and sophisticated language of the "experts" who always seem to know best, or manipulated by the carefully arranged "leaks" or semiofficial, anonymous "backgrounders" by bureaucrats seeking to influence public opinion in support of predetermined decisions.

THIS IS AN INTOLERABLE SITUATION for a government founded on the premise that in order to succeed it must have the active and full participation of an enlightened electorate. That is what our forefathers attempted to ensure when they created a government of laws rather than of men and enshrined the distinction in a written Constitution. That, too, is why they insisted upon attaching a Bill of Rights to the Constitution, guaranteeing maximum competition in the marketplace of ideas. Today, however, we find ourselves victims of a system in which adopted policies often have neither the knowledge nor the approval of the people, and are the decisions of a minority of elites and elected officials.

Can anyone, for example, doubt that our present system of document classification is a farce, and an expensive one at that? The practice of stamping public papers with some sort of secrecy designation has become so widespread as to be virtually meaningless. In testimony before a June 1971 hearing of the House of Representatives' Foreign Operations and Government Information Subcommittee, William G. Florence, a retired civilian security classification policy expert on Department of Defense procedures for classification, claimed that "less than one-half of 1%" of the millions of documents bearing classification markings actually contain information qualifying for even the lowest authorized classification. "In other words," Florence contended, "the disclosure of information in at least 99½% of these classified documents could not be prejudicial to the defense interest of the nation." He later increased his estimate of the number of documents that need to be protected from 1% to 5%, but the point of his testimony remains the same.

Following what seems to be a philosophy of "when in doubt, classify," tens of thousands of government employees routinely exercise their delegated authority to deny the public access to information through the simple use of a rubber stamp and ink pad, tempered only by the classifier's own imperfect subjective interpretation of vague classification guidelines.

During the 1970s, the classification practices of the departments of Defense and State and the Atomic Energy Commission, alone, reportedly involved some 38,000 persons and have resulted in the secreting away of more than 22 million documents. Most other government agencies also have authority to either use or originate classified information. Indeed, the authority to classify has become a liberally dispensed privilege rather than a limited and controlled responsibility, as intended. Items such as interoffice memos, backgrounders, and public policy documents are classified more frequently for the dubious purpose of bolstering a sagging sense of self-importance or of "playing it safe" by providing a degree of protection for the classifier's possible poor judgment or the author's unsubstantiated criticisms or questionable recommendations, than as the result of a studied determination indicating that release of the material would be harmful to the nation's security.

But if the excesses of government classification are outlandish, the abuses of executive privilege are outrageous. Information required by Congress, if it is to perform its duties intelligently, is regularly and somewhat self-righteously withheld, enabling any administration to make momentous and often irreversible decisions without the discipline of congressional review, the benefit of congressional advice, or the need for legislative endorsement.

THE RIGHT OF CONGRESS to demand and receive information from executive officials must supersede the prerogative of those men and women to keep their secrets secret: I consider the ease and frequency with which members of the administration hide behind the protective cloak of executive privilege to be an affront to the people who elected the members of Congress to represent their interests. It is an insulting expression of either disdain or mistrust of individual congressmen or for congressional operations as a whole, and is an indication of the low regard held by the executive for the legislative branch's status as an equal and independent arm of government.

The entire concept of executive privilege carries with it the undemocratic connotation of some sort of kingly divine right. However, it is more of a tradition than a right and should either be discontinued or defined and legitimatized by statute. Certainly the practice of permitting anyone other than the president to initiate such a practice must be stopped. Actually there is no constitutional or legislative authority for either the government's classification procedures or the doctrine of executive privilege. They have evolved out of executive order or assumption and have been more or less accepted as custom, although they are a clear contradiction to an open government and the freedom of information concept.

The dispute among government, and citizens, and the executive and Congress over what information can and will be made available has been going on in varying degrees of intensity ever since President Washington opened the controversy by turning down a congressional request for information on an expedition into the Northwest Territories. As might be expected, most practices of government secrecy and censorship evolved out of what has been considered the necessity of maintaining military security during wartime. The Civil War prompted direct military censorship for the first time in the nation's history and led to a major confrontation with the principle of a free press when Union zealots used it as a device to seize or suppress opposition newspapers and even to jail editors who dared differ with the war's conduct or its goals.

Perhaps because this sounded a warning bell in the minds of many believers of the sanctity of a free press, an uneasy partnership was achieved between the news media and government during the two world wars. President Wilson created a Committee on Public Information in 1917, and President Roosevelt established the Office of Censorship in 1941, each affording the press an opportunity to have some voice, albeit severely limited, in the censorship of those eras.

Even in wartime, however, no attempt to pass a law abridging the constitutionally guaranteed freedom of the press has ever succeeded in passing Congress. The problem has been that, although wartime conditions admittedly make it necessary to be cautious about the possible disclosure of information that might compromise national security, the practices of suppression once planted and rationalized, for whatever reason, usually persist long after the purported need is gone.

The reason so many of today's secrecy practices have gone largely unchallenged can easily be traced back to World War II, when the people were conditioned to believe "the enemy has ears everywhere" and that "loose lips sink ships." There was little, if any, public news media resistance to the government's contention that strict censorship was required to maintain our security and protect "our men in uniform." Never mind the fact that the suppression of information was often carried to absurd extremes; it would have been considered unpatriotic to argue the point, especially during wartime. Although the war ended, unfortunately the culture of secrecy did not. The indoctrination of the American people was so successful, in fact, that it was easy for the government to carry it forward to the cold war and to expand it from purely military information to matters of public policy.

Because Congress has consistently balked at assuming responsibility for enacting legislation and defining and limiting what government materials can be classified, establishment of classification guidelines has become, by default, the prerogative of the executive. This has been exercised in a series of executive orders, some less vague and suppressive than others, but none of which has proved to be acceptable.

President Truman's Executive Order 10290 of September 24, 1951, prescribing minimum standards for the classification and handling of publications "which require safeguarding in the interest of the security of the United States," was widely criticized for being too favorable to government and for its lack of adequate review or appeals procedures.

On November 5, 1953, President Eisenhower replaced the Truman directive with Executive Order 10501 intended to bring about "a proper balance between the need to protect information important to the defense of the United States and the need for citizens of this country to know what this country is doing." Initially praised by proponents of greater access to government information for its imposition of review and appeal procedures and its reduction of classification categories, the Eisenhower Administration was later the object of severe public and news media criticism for failing to live up to its promise. Acting outside our system of checks and balances as both judge and jury of its own executive order, the administration, then as now, liberally and self-servingly interpreted the doctrine to withhold information that, to many, did not seem to fall into the three categories set forth and defined below.

1. Top secret: "Information or material the defense aspect of which is paramount, and the unauthorized disclosure of which could result in exceptionally grave damage to the nation, such as leading to a definite break in diplomatic relations affecting the defense of the United States, an armed attack against the United States or its allies, a war, or the compromise of military or defense plans or intelligence operations, or scientific or technological developments vital to national defense."

2. Secret: "Defense information or material the unauthorized disclosure of which could result in serious damage to the nation, such as jeopardizing the international relations of the United States, endangering the effectiveness of a program of policy of vital importance to the national defense, or compromising important military or defense plans, scientific or technological developments important to national defense, or information revealing important intelligence operations."

3. Confidential: "Defense information or material the unauthorized disclosure of which could be prejudicial to the defense interests of the nation."

THESE GUIDELINES MAY SEEM REASONABLE and even justifiable upon first examination, but the tests of time and experience have shown that the impreciseness of language and the absence of specific declassification provisions open the way for the inclusion of practically any materials the classifier desires and for as long as it serves the government's rather than the public's interests.

President Kennedy attempted to correct some of the failings of the government's classification system when he issued Executive Order 10964 in 1961, providing that, "When classified information or material no longer requires its present level of protection in the defense interest, it shall be downgraded in order to preserve the effectiveness and integrity of the classification system and to eliminate classifications of information or material which no longer require classification protection." It was a step in the right direction, but to my mind, it fails to solve the declassification dilemma because it places the cart before the horse. The automatic release of materials should be provided for at the time of classification, not years later, and should be strictly adhered to unless an appropriate, independent review body can be convinced by the arguments of the affected agency that there are compelling reasons for extending the period of classification protection beyond the normally stipulated disclosure date.

It must also be recognized that government not only has erected barriers to protect its own self-construed secrets from the public, but also has adopted the role of receptacle, guardian, and perpetuator of corporate secrecy. Information that, if made public, would provide consumers with the knowledge needed to detect and respond to the injustices and illegalities inflicted upon them by business-corporate interests is collected by government officials and placed under cover while citizen continue to be victimized in the market place.

In 1966, President Johnson signed into law the highly touted Freedom of Information Act, designed to force federal agencies to make available to the public more of their carefully-hoarded information. Over the opposition of the affected agencies and like-minded business interests, the measure largely rewrote Section 3 of the 1946 Administrative Procedure Act to require the release of all agency data, unless specifically exempted. But therein lies the rub. The scope of the nine exempted categories, included to overcome the objections of the act's opponents [a classic example of a bipartisan compromise], is so broad as to enable the government to withhold almost as much material from the public as before. In fact, V. M. Newton, Jr., a founder of the Freedom of Information movement, called the nine following exemptions "nothing more than an open invitation to the federal bureaucrat to withhold legitimate information from the American people":

Material "specifically required by executive order to be kept secret in the interest of the national defense or foreign policy"

Material related "solely" to agencies' internal personnel rules and practices

Material specifically exempted from disclosure by statute

Privileged or confidential trade secrets or financial information

Inter- or intra-agency memoranda or letters which would be unavailable by law to a person in litigation with the agency

Personnel and medical files "the disclosure of which would constitute a clearly unwarranted invasion of personal privacy"

Investigatory files compiled for law enforcement except to the extent available by law to private parties.

Material contained in or related to examination reports of agencies regulating financial institutions

Geological and geophysical information and data, including maps concerning wells or condition

As Robert O. Blanchard, former head of the communication department at American University, commented, "Several of the phrases seem bound to encourage continued, perhaps more sophisticated, federal agency discretion in release of information."

Ideally, however, I believe the entire Freedom of Information (FOI) law should be revoked, and only information covered by direct executive order or specifically exempted from disclosure by statute should be granted the right of secrecy. Even this should be done sparingly and under close supervision.

THE CONTROVERSY OF THE PENTAGON PAPERS, as perhaps no other single event in modern history, served to dramatize what little progress, if any, was made by the nation toward achieving its espoused goal of an open government and how contemptuously the citizen's right to know has been regarded. The calculated practices of deceit, distortion, and denial of information, exposed by the contents of this remarkable study, made possible the commission of a monstrous crime upon the American people: the waging of an unnecessary, undeclared war in a foreign land and the reprehensible usurping of congressional powers.

Without the carefully orchestrated public and political attitudes fashioned by a succession of purposefully isolated administrations utilizing the twin tools of propaganda and secrecy, I do not believe the people of this nation would have condoned the decisions made and the policies implemented. Surely, had the ordinary citizen been privy to the information and, yes, the thinking so jealously restricted to the uppermost echelons of government, our ill-conceived involvement in Southeast Asia, with its resultant and irrecoverable costs in lives, social progress, and world credibility, would never have been permitted to run its tragic course.

The abrogation of the people's right to know—one of our system's most important checks and balances—caused this nation to make this colossal mistake of waging a war that has nothing to do with our security individually or as a nation. The crime, therefore, surrounding the public disclosure of the *Pentagon Papers* is not, as the Nixon Administration would have us believe, that Dr. Daniel Ellsberg released these materials to the press or that *The New York Times, Boston Globe, Washington Post,* and other newspapers proceeded to publish them. The real travesty of justice is that the study was classified at all; that it became necessary to circumvent the executive's self-imposed shroud of secrecy in order to convey to the public information which was rightfully theirs all along.

What better proof is needed to refute the Nixon Administration's claim that the release of the *Pentagon Papers* constituted some sort of shocking moral and legal crime, endangering national security, than the *Papers* themselves, in page after page spelling out in chilling detail how badly the people had been misled. I became convinced that this information had to be made public.

On the day before my filibuster was to start to make public the *Pentagon Papers*, at President Nixon's direction, the Pentagon delivered an official copy of the entire study to the leaders of Congress. Special conditions limited access to the material to members of Congress. No staff members were allowed in the special reading room, and the nation's legislators, in the presence of a guard, were prohibited from taking notes. It infuriated me to see Congress, which is supposed to make policy for this country, submit to such demeaning rules.

For too long Congress had played along in keeping secrets from the people. To do it again, in the midst of this crucial test of the people's right to know, was an abdication of its own power, a condoning of Nixon's act of suppression.

People have asked me if I had it to do over, would I go through the ordeal again. I have answered many times that I am convinced the lessons to be learned from the *Pentagon Papers* outweighed by far any possible risk. I hoped by that action I would help shorten by even one day, the senseless killing and destruction in Southeast Asia. And I hoped that it would penetrate the shroud of secrecy enveloping and protecting our highest echelons of government. Given the same set of circumstances, I would do it again. Secrecy is democracy's worst enemy.

THE LIES OF GOVERNMENT officialdom are difficult to stomach. As one example, in 1969, I received a letter from a distinguished professor of political science at the University of Alaska in Fairbanks, Dr. Richard Feinberg, claiming he had discovered that the Army was conducting nerve gas tests on a nearby military installation. "I thought you should be made aware of this," he wrote.

Dr. Feinberg knew of my intense opposition to the continuing development and stockpiling of lethal gases by this country and of my persistent efforts to convince the administration to seek Senate ratification of the long-pending Geneva Protocol, already signed by practically every other major power in the world, banning the use of all deadly chemicals as weapons of war. He rightly assumed I would not be too pleased to learn that nerve gas tests were being conducted in my own state.

I immediately contacted a high-ranking Department of the Army official and asked point blank, "Is there any poisonous gas testing being conducted anywhere in Alaska?" The answer was as clear as the question, "Absolutely not."

In my naiveté (I had been a U.S. Senator for only a few months), I accepted this official declaration in good faith and informed Dr. Feinberg that I was sure he would be as delighted as I to learn that he had been mistaken. Less than a month later, Dr. Feinberg succeeded in documenting his charges sufficiently for the Army to finally concede "some" nerve gas experiments had indeed taken place in Alaska. In short, the Army official lied to me.

CANNIKIN NUCLEAR TESTING—ANOTHER EXAMPLE. The government's handling of the five detonations leading up to a five-megaton underground nuclear explosion on Alaska's Amchitka Island on November 6, 1971, for example, was steeped in secrecy and distinguished by an apparent disregard for the legitimate concerns of millions of Americans, as well as those of friendly nations, such as Canada and Japan. Secrecy surrounded not only the need for the test, but the very basis on which the government decided the question of safety. Internal reports containing environmental arguments against the test were deliberately denied the advantage of public examination and congressional debate. Court action finally succeeded in prying loose some of these adverse comments, but it never brought them all into the open; and what was achieved was too late for the public to consider them adequately.

Not only has vital public information surrounding the Amchitka tests been kept secret since the program originated, but the Atomic Energy Commission (AEC) went so far as to conduct a deliberate and expensive campaign to discredit anyone daring to question or oppose its series of underground nuclear explosions.

After the 1969 detonation of the Milrow blast, which I also opposed, the AEC, through its prime contractor, actually opened up a publicity and public relations office in Anchorage and sent out press handouts and public speakers throughout Alaska which, in McCarthyism style, impugned the motivations and questioned the loyalty of myself and anyone else in opposition to the AEC position. One of the actual statements made, and published in a newspaper of wide circulation in Alaska, was that those opposing the planned atomic test Cannikin were "part of an international conspiracy to impede the defense posture of our country."

So here we have a case where not only was public information kept secret, but an elected public official was attacked with public funds for assuming the role of adversary on a vital public issue.

Even today, it is premature for anyone to claim that the 1971 Amchitka Cannikin blast was an unqualified success. Only the test of time can accurately make that determination. Although there fortunately was no immediate catastrophe, as many feared, the possibility exists that the risky detonation deep under the surface of that Aleutian island might well have planted nuclear seeds of destruction yet to be reaped. The cavity created by the blast caused a distortion of the earth's crust which, like a nuclear time bomb, could still act as a trigger for larger-than-natural earthquakes. And the probable leakage of radioactivity into the surrounding ocean for decades to come presents a continuing danger to vulnerable marine life and the food chain of the North Pacific.

THE CONCERN I HAVE over whether the right decision was made is aggravated by the secret manner in which it was made. An act of great potential danger, involving both life and the environment, was undertaken; and the people were precluded from participating in that decision. When the executive department suppresses the internal debate surrounding a public issue, the citizen is left with little by which to judge the government's decision.

The difficulty in obtaining the release of the environmental impact study relating to the Amchitka Cannikin test, for example, was said to be that it was considered a part of a larger classified report concerning the test's purpose of developing a more powerful anti-ballistic missile warhead. The practice of taking a public report, unrelated to national defense by any stretch of the imagination, and incorporating it as part of a national defense document so the entire work can then be classified must be stopped.

After Cannikin, the second detonation of the five planned, I received leaked information that the testing was for a safeguard missile warhead that had been declared obsolete by the military. Once I made this information public, the balance of the tests was stopped and the private contractors dismissed.

SOLUTIONS: AN INDEPENDENT BOARD. Most importantly, the standards for protective classification of information must be revised and the public's right to have access to available information and thinking on matters relating to its security and survival is too critical to be sacrificed to a decision-making process shrouded in secrecy and immune from the light of public examination.

An independent board, including representatives from the legislative and judicial branches of government, with a majority of the members representing the public sector, should be established to study the present practices of classification, to establish new and more liberal procedures, and to recommend needed legislation. The executive branch should not be represented on this board; rather it should be required to plead its case for secrecy before the appointed board.

Any future standards for classification should be weighed heavily in favor of the public's right to know. Indeed, the public should not have to prove its need for information; the government should be made to justify any request it makes for the withholding of information. Better we err on the side of freedom of information than on the side of suppression. If this entails some risk, so be it. Freedom is impossible without risk, and certainly the risks of free discussion are less to be feared than the risks of repression.

Automatic time limits should be an integral part of any items which are classified. All classified documents should be declassified as a matter of course after two years, unless the classifications board approves a government request for an extension of secrecy. The board would be empowered to send relevant papers to the appropriate committees of

Congress at any time and to serve as an appellate on declassification disputes.

One of the board's most urgent tasks would be to press for revision or repeal of Executive Order 10501. At a minimum, specific language is required to ensure that the classification system is applied only to information that, if disclosed, would definitely compromise our national defense posture. At the same time, it is essential to make certain no other item can be haphazardly lumped into the system unless it meets these criteria.

One of the greatest ironies and dangers of the secrecy syndrome is that people sometimes fail to distinguish between the desirability of having all of government's activities made public and the necessity for protecting the individual's right to privacy.

"All of us have our secrets," they reason, "so why shouldn't the government be entitled to its secrets as well?" This feeling is largely a product of the conditioning imposed upon us by our competitive enterprise system, which relies heavily on confidentiality and trade secrets. The public has been told so often and so convincingly that government and business have the right not only to keep certain matters secret, but to acquire information by secret means as well, that it has come to accept such practices as an integral part of the system.

Nonsense! The individual has a constitutional right to privacy, while the government has a constitutional obligation to inform. The proposed board on secrecy, therefore, should have control over not only the classification of information, but also the shameful manner in which such material is often gathered.

In 1971, for instance, it was revealed that thousands of members of the armed forces intelligence branches had been engaged, and hundreds of millions of dollars spent over several years so that the military could spy on civilians, federal agencies could keep tabs on one another, the privacy of the citizen could be invaded, and the rights of the First Amendment could be compromised. Yet even Congress seems unable to secure information on such subjects as Army surveillance of civilians or mushrooming databank programs. Indeed, the gigantic nature of our state and corporate society, with all its demand for record keeping, makes it literally impossible for anyone, even if he wished it, to live the life of a recluse.

I believe it is this kind of atmosphere, which has developed slowly, almost invisibly, and to some extent unintentionally, that has increasingly made it easier and easier for those who argue for more and more irrelevant snooping into our private lives. The degree to which government and big business pry into matters which are purely our private affairs, and which have no possible bearing on national security, is staggering.

Stopping this reckless, and recklessly growing, practice may be the single most vital need of all those requiring immediate attention, for if we lose control of our privacy, which is in effect to lose control of ourselves, we are prisoners. And there is very little that prisoners can do to bring about change.

THE GROWING USE OF WIRETAPPING is especially disquieting. Under the broad cover of "national interest," the Justice Department admits that it has frequently used wiretaps to gather evidence. The seemingly irrepressible growth of this gross invasion of privacy becomes even more dramatic, and more frightening, when one realizes that since the legal concept of the "inviolate personality" was introduced in 1890 by Samuel D. Warren and Louis D. Brandeis, the right to privacy was recognized and supposedly protected by more than 35 state legislative enactments and over 400 Supreme Court decisions.

How then do we account for such phenomena as the conclusion of Aryeh Neier, Executive Director of the American Civil Liberties Union, wrote in his study of the dissemination of derogatory data by the FBI, that "At the very least, millions of people have been injured by data dissemination functions that the FBI has taken on which go beyond the Bureau's legislative authority"?

Using data drawn from federal court records in the 1971 case of *Menard v. Mitchell and Hoover,* Neier reported that in 1970 the FBI received an average of 29,000 sets of fingerprints per working day, of which 16,000 came from non-law enforcement agencies such as banks, insurance companies, and government agencies engaged in employing or licensing people. Upon receipt of these fingerprints, standard procedure "was to report to the submitting agency the material in the FBI files on the person fingerprinted."

The trouble is a great deal of this data is raw and unverified. For example, although nearly half of all arrests for actions other than traffic violations do not result in convictions, there is no indication on arrest records whether the arrested person was ever convicted.

Yet because the FBI has almost no control over what happens to this information once it sends it out, these records are inevitably acquired by the multi-tentacled credit industry. In a report undertaken for the ACLU, Ralph Nader stated that the Association of Credit Bureaus of America (ACBA) keeps 105 million files. "These economic interests have almost total control over the information they collect and sell," reports Nader. "They are not accountable to anyone except those who seek to purchase the information. Further, for reasons of profit, these companies place a premium on the derogatory information they assemble."

An arrest record, as noted in the *Menard* case by the U.S. Circuit Court of Appeals for the District of Columbia, "may subject an individual to serious difficulties. Opportunities for schooling, employment, or professional licenses may be restricted or non-existent as a consequence of the mere fact of an arrest, even if followed by acquittal or complete exoneration." The court cited a survey showing that 75% of New York area employment agencies would not accept for referral an applicant with an arrest record. Another survey of 75 employers showed that 66 of them would not consider hiring a man who had been acquitted of an arrest for assault.

Dogged by an arrest record for victim and victimless crimes, a record that follows him even if charges were dropped or he was acquitted or never prosecuted, a citizen in today's tightly intertwined society finds the doors closed to credit, bank loans, mortgages, apartment rentals, licenses, and admission to schools. Moreover, because the FBI does not differentiate between juvenile and adult records, a minor youthful misstep can have the same crushing consequences. They can, indeed, twist the entire future of a young life.

With all these doors shut to an arrest victim, doors which control access to nearly all the necessities and amenities of life in 20th Century

America, it is no wonder some people slip into a life of crime and thoughtful people cry out against the "dossier dictatorship." It is logical to ask, as Neier does in concluding his study,

> Is crime being controlled or reduced by the dissemination of this data? It would be more reasonable to say that the FBI's data dissemination policies have served to increase crime. Once people have been denied jobs, licenses, homes, admissions to schools and credit, the likelihood that they will commit crimes would seem to rise rather than fall.

CLEARLY, THE TIME IS LONG OVERDUE for severe controls to be clamped on the dossier industry, both inside and outside of government. Strict requirements must be placed on the information that can be placed in them in the first place. Why should the FBI collect data on anyone other than persons convicted of a crime or fugitives from some law enforcement agency? Juvenile records must be clearly marked as such. The dossiers should be available only to law enforcement agencies and those needing the material for judging sentencing, probation or parole. Finally, since it was the cloak of secrecy, which enabled the FBI to follow such promiscuous practices of data dissemination in the first place, legislation must be enacted to provide for thorough public scrutiny of the Bureau's practices.

The FBI is by no means the only agency whose practices constitute a threat to our vital right to privacy; some 20 federal agencies are engaged in intelligence activities. Among them are the Internal Revenue Service, the Post Office, the Secret Service, the Customs Bureau, the Civil Service Commission (which lists 15 million—repeat, 15 million—names of "subversive activity" suspects), the Immigration and Naturalization Service, the Passport Office, the so-called anti-subversive committees in Congress, and the military services. The Army itself has admitted that in the late 1960s it had 1,200 agents doing the field work for a large staff which operated a dossier bank of 25 million "personalities."

This was a good deal of the work I did during my tour of duty in the Counter Intelligence Corps in the early 1950s. I trust it might be fair to guess that if anyone ever took the trouble to tabulate all the millions of persons on file in the millions of dossiers in all these branches of government, over half the citizens of America are in some kind of file for some kind of irrelevant reason. Add to this the millions more who are on file in state and local intelligence offices, and the threat to the health of our free society is self-evident.

In testimony before the Senate in 1971, Burt Neuborne, an attorney for the ACLU, stated it this way: "The chilling effect of pervasive surveillance will inevitably destroy any society's capacity for dissent, non-conformity and heterodoxy. Subtract those elements from a libertarian democracy and you have totalitarianism."

The existing method for undertaking any such surveillance under law or by executive action should be ended and the laws changed to make it unlawful for whatever reason by anyone, government or private.

Fourth Amendment protections against unreasonable search and seizure gave some degree of safety to Americans before the technological revolution. But with today's profusion of sophisticated photographic and electronic devices for bugging and wiretapping, a pervasive sense of being watched can stifle the spontaneity without which a free society can slide into a police state mentality.

Furthermore, the military must get completely out of the business of snooping on civilians, and all their intelligence dossiers now in existence must be destroyed. All data collection on persons engaged in lawful political activity, no matter how controversial, must be absolutely prohibited. The same ban must be strictly applied to the current practice of storing (and, too often, disseminating) hearsay, anonymous, derogatory information about individuals. As I said earlier, the careless dissemination of arrest records is a practice which can fence a person off from society; strict limitations must be placed on their use. Furthermore, a statute of limitations must be enacted regarding the use of arrest records and other information so citizens can make a fresh start in a social sense, just as bankruptcy proceedings permit persons to make a fresh start in their economic lives.

There are still other safeguards which must be enacted to maintain a free and open society against the surveillance menace. Every person about whom personal data is being stored by the government or by such organizations as credit bureaus must be notified of that fact and permitted to check his dossier for accuracy. Individuals must have the right to challenge the veracity of material in their dossiers. They must also have the right to challenge dissemination of material in their dossiers to anyone or any agency, meaning they must be notified whenever anyone is seeking information from their dossiers. When procedural safeguards are violated, individuals should be able to recover damages.

Unfortunately, the democracy-emasculating practices of secrecy are by no means limited in government to the executive branch. While deploring the executive's penchant for secrecy, Congress abets the system by docilely honoring the executive classification of documents and retaining such data behind its closed committee doors. Only on rare occasions is such information "leaked" to the press or otherwise passed along to the public.

The foregoing text was written 37 years ago. The problem I described then is considerably worse today. The answer is not "politics as usual" in the Congress, the Judiciary or the Executive, all which are complicit in our unfortunate state of affairs. Permit me to share some shocking information that relates to the results of our War on Drugs and our justice system's extensive use of incarceration for victimless crimes. I compared, on a per capita basis, the number of people in prison in Germany just before the beginning of World War II to the number of Americans we have in prison today. The per capita comparison reveals that we have six times more people in jail than Hitler had in Germany in 1938. What this comparison reveals about the present state of our free society is shocking.

THE PENTAGON PAPERS STORY DID NOT END with my reading and placing them into public record. When media lost their nerve and refused to publish the entire *Pentagon Papers*, I had arranged for their private publication with Beacon Press (the publishing arm of the Unitarian Universalist Association), the only publisher in the United States that would take on the risk in view of the Supreme Court decision on the day I released the *Papers*, putting further publication of the *Papers* at risk.

A grand jury investigating violations of federal law subpoenaed one of my aides. As an intervener, I moved to quash the subpoena, contending that it would violate the Speech or Debate Clause of the Constitution to compel my aide to testify. The District Court denied the motion. The Court of Appeals affirmed the denial. The Supreme Court in *Gravel v United States* decided the case on a 5-4 vote, providing immunity from prosecution for me for acts operating within the confines of the Senate, based on the Speech or Debate Clause. The four minority justices felt I had immunity under the clause wherever I exercised speech. Essentially the Court ruled that members of Congress enjoy immunity to release any classified information to the American people—a decision still operable today.

Since that ruling, no member of Congress has found anything of a classified nature to reveal to the public. This lapse of Congressional responsibility was not noticeable until May 2007 when Senator Dick Durbin (D-IL) explained, as a matter of conscience, why he in 2002, along with other lawmakers on the Intelligence Committee, failed to make public the differences in intelligence briefings they were receiving about Iraqi weapons of mass destruction and the case based on the same intelligence information the White House was making for war to America and the rest of the world.

Senator Durbin said he was conflicted about revealing intelligence information that was different from what the Bush Administration was saying to the American public fearing his revelation would cause loss of life in the intelligence-gathering network. Tragically, had he made his knowledge public prior to the vote on October 11, 2002, it might have been sufficient to stop the run up to the war and thwart the Democratic support of the Lieberman resolution that gave Bush the power to go to war. Durbin did vote against the war resolution.

Senator Durbin should be commended for his act of conscience in revealing this information now, but had he been aware of the Supreme Court decision, he might have acted differently; and American history might have taken a different course. Nevertheless, he now suffers a moral conflict that by keeping quiet, the lead up to the war was never challenged, and now there has been an extreme loss of life.

A POSTSCRIPT TO THE CANNIKIN NUCLEAR TEST: Seven years ago, I was contacted by the wife of one of the miners who dug the mile-deep shaft for the Cannikin test. She called to apologize for opposing my efforts to stop the testing. She had been a secretary with the Laborers union that fought my efforts; stopping the tests obviously threatened their jobs.

When the shaft on Amchitka was sealed in preparation for the detonation of the atomic bomb, there was no accounting for a lost canister of cesium. This loss was known to the authorities who were safely at sea in a Navy vessel during the blast; yet the detonation was ordered to proceed. All of the miners who had worked in the shaft and were there at the site on the island at the time of detonation died within five to 10 years of various types of cancer.

Because the unusual number of deaths, the government quickly paid the widows of the dead miners $150,000 each. When the missing cesium was exposed by non-government scientists, the government made another payment to the widows of $125,000 in hopes of silencing criticism of the whole affair—government officialdom at work.

THESE ANECDOTAL EXPERIENCES of one elected official are closer to the norm than the exception. Specific foreign aid planning documents, CIA expenditures, overseas military commitments, our clandestine activities in various parts of the world, the worldwide deployment of nuclear weapons, environmental studies, agreements related to nuclear power plants, and many other "government papers" have been systematically treated as "sacred cows" by the executive, not to be defiled by the inquiring eyes of even a congressional committee, much less the people. Yet the Congress must pass upon, and the public is expected to accept, legislation founded almost solely upon the unsubstantiated requirements of an uncommunicative military-industrial establishment that claims "national security" and tight-lipped administrations that assert "executive privilege."

If it is painful for citizens to accept the fact that they are not being provided with all the information they need to properly judge their government's actions, imagine how frustrating it is for United States senators to discover they too, are unable to secure the material necessary for the proper discharge of their legislative responsibilities or, even worse, that they are deliberately lied to or misled.

With a brief glimpse of the record of the early 1970s, is it any wonder that after 9/11, fear and vengeance were the political tools used by the political elites running our government to further threaten our democracy? The lead up to the Iraq War has been an outright fraud on the American people. The Congress has proven itself impotent to correct or end this tragedy. The Iraq War is a total *deja vu* of the Vietnam War. The rhetoric of our political leadership centers on the fact that the mistake—the invasion and its aftermath—was incompetently executed. Where would we be if the mistake were competently executed? As General Sanchez admitted, we invaded Iraq to get their oil and we are not about to leave and lose control of their oil—actions totally in accord with American imperialistic policies. But these are not the policies of a real democracy.

Few in Congress really understood the full ramifications of the Patriot Act when it was passed in a panic. That legislation in great detail reinforces everything that was attempted earlier by government forces seeking to control the polity and now their power is officially in place.

It is fantasy to think that "politics as usual" will correct this forward movement of the demise of our democracy. There are only two alternatives that can change the status quo: 1) the government, wherein lies the problem, with an electoral process steeped in "politics as usual," or 2) the American people, empowered to make laws that those in representative government find impossible to enact. As I pointed out in Chapter 2, the people can correct this error through the use of the National Initiative—the empowerment of the people to make laws, working in partnership with their elected officials.

The End of Secrecy

Secrecy is democracy's worst enemy.

Government uses the tools of "national security" and "executive privilege" to keep the public and Congress in the dark about government decision-making and to thwart accountability.

Executive privilege is an affront to the public and their elected officials, who need information from executive officials to carry out their duties.

Fear conditions the public to unquestioningly accept the government's secrecy practices.

The entire Freedom of Information (FOI) law should be revoked; only information covered by direct executive order or statute should be granted the right of secrecy.

An independent board—excluding the executive branch— should be established to study the current practices of classification, establish new and more liberal procedures, and recommend needed legislation.

The individual has a constitutional right to privacy; the government has a constitutional obligation to inform the public.

It is vital that we end the government's practice of prying into purely private matters of its citizens.

The time is long overdue to establish strict controls on the dossier industry, both inside and outside of government.

The military must get completely out of the business of snooping on civilians, and all of their intelligence dossiers now in existence must be destroyed.

Change can come from only two alternatives: 1) the government, wherein lies the problem, or 2) the American people, if they are empowered to make laws to limit the invasion of our privacy, as outlined in Chapter 2.

10

American Imperialism

Of all the evils to public liberty, war is perhaps the most
to be dreaded, because it comprises and develops every other.
War is the parent of armies; from those proceed debts and taxes.
And armies and debts, and taxes, are the known
instruments for bringing the many under the domination
of the few. In war, too, the discretionary power of the
executive is extended; its influence in dealing out offices,
honors, and emoluments is multiplied; and all the means
of seducing the minds are added to those of
subduing the force of the people!
James Madison

IN THE AFTERMATH of World War II, several changes of enormous significance were made in American domestic and foreign policy. It was decided to keep the draft in peacetime, despite a 175-year tradition in America against all forms of conscription. Massive espionage and secret police organs, developed during the pressures of World War II, were kept and expanded. After the troop reduction at the end of the war, a great military build-up was begun, with ever increasing military budgets for increasingly costly and fancier weapon systems. The first two-million-man standing army in America's peacetime history and an economy anxious for the presumed stability that comes from "defense expenditures" led to the construction of a "warfare state" capable of garrisoning the world.

The establishment of the National Security Council, and the Truman Doctrine, containing communism, made America the world's police force (a policy carried on to this day even though the Soviet Union has imploded and communism is no longer a threat anywhere in the world). Congressional criticism of foreign affairs did not go beyond the water's edge. All these formal and informal policies meant no questions were to be asked of the military. The result was the continued "bipartisanship" support for the war industry machine, which muted constructive analysis and criticism of our postwar foreign activities. The development of an American "warfare state" also meant that grievous problems at home went unattended. Domestic priorities were directed away from people's needs and skewed to the defense establishment—the military-industrial complex—a situation that haunts us to this day as the rationale for defense becomes ever more preemptive.

This institutional transformation was achieved without a change in the Constitution. It was achieved largely without public debate and with little public notice. It amounts to a *coup d'etat* that has militarized American culture. No major elections were won or lost on these issues, no extensive debate was carried on in Congress; but the government buildup brought about by the cold war changed the focus of American political power.

Side by side with this change in the government mission came the global expansion of the American corporation—the maturation of economic globalization. The U.S. military set up bases around the world to protect our "vital interests." Military interest supported corporate interests around the world. The sole superpower, the United States, is now the sole global imperial power.

Domestically, senior military men, defense bureaucrats, defense industry executives, retired officers in and out of Congress, and scholars paid by defense contracts worked together in a climate of shared interests in weapons, standing forces, real or imagined threats, and protracted conflict. They have now become an interlocking self-serving directorate for American militarism as they replace each other at the top of the hierarchies of power. Their prophecies of conflict become self-fulfilling, as they induce the very international maneuvers which feed their power positions. Just as an unchecked rivalry in arms led directly to World War I, so there is a large element of truth in American sociologist C.

Wright Mills' statement that the "immediate cause of World War III is the preparation for it."

Although there has been corruption in this military-industrial complex, the corruption is not as frightening as much as the built-in lobby for war, for preparations for war, and against domestic priorities. As constituencies dependent on defense industries are broadened, the critical faculties of the citizenry are dulled, neutralizing one of the key checks on the power and growth of the military-industrial complex. The constitutional checks and balances within the federal government, the rights of states, and a critical citizenry have all been eroded by this great change in the American political and economic power constellation.

It is prescient and instructive that America's two foremost military leaders who later became presidents warned us of foreign military entanglements—George Washington and Dwight Eisenhower. In the latter's farewell address, President Eisenhower called attention to "the conjunction of an immense military establishment and a large arms industry" and warned the nation to "guard against the acquisition of unwarranted influence, whether sought or unsought, by the military-industrial complex. The potential for the disastrous rise of misplaced power exists and will persist." No president since, has even acknowledged the problem. We failed to heed the warnings of these great leaders and now the dimensions of our warfare state are appalling.

The raw size of the defense budget is a large part of the problem. Between 10% and 15% of the federal budget during the 1930s went for national defense; in the 1960s the range was 55% to 65%, in spite of a great expansion of social progress in the intervening years. This reflected an increase in annual outlays of $750 million in the early 1930s to $1 billion in 1939 to $77 billion in 1970 and more than $650 billion in 2007.

At the height of the Cold War, we spent on the defense establishment $400 for every man, woman, and child in America. By comparison, the Soviet Union spent only $230 (in equivalent purchasing power per capita); Great Britain, $100; France, $123; West Germany, $103; and the People's Republic of China, $9! We are indeed "first in the world"—first in overkill, first in wasteful extravagance, and first in irrational fear of foreign enemies.

109

All this is no accident. These huge sums not only make possible the continuation of a runaway warfare state, but they also serve an important economic function that wins them the support of the business-corporate constituency. Most advanced industrialized economies now require a large public sector for the stabilization of aggregate demand, and in the United States this has been most easily achieved through a large defense sector. Once the mechanism is created, of course, it becomes in the interest of all those in the defense sector that there be an uninterrupted, and preferably expanding, flow of public money into it. Policies, programs, and attitudes that support and reinforce that flow are looked upon as good in themselves, and those that don't are strenuously opposed. The momentum is great, and the constituency large.

Businessmen and chambers of commerce (both of whom are regularly romanced by the military with fully-paid junkets to military installations) regularly rant against the dangers of socialism, and a large public sector regularly excludes all defense spending from their condemnation. Yet it is this category of government spending that has increased most markedly in the past 50 years.

It is not surprising that supervision of expenditures has been woefully deficient in the defense industry. Uniformed officers meant to watchdog public defense contracts soon become captive of the very firms they are supposed to oversee. Retired officers inhabit the executive halls of the defense corporations with non-jobs that have more to do with whom they still know on active duty or in public office than with any particular "technical expertise" they might bring to the firm. A congressional study several years ago found that some 2,000 retired military officers of the rank of colonel or Navy captain and above were employed by the 100 largest defense contractors holding two-thirds of the contracts. Almost one-fourth of this number (465) were former military officers employed by the nine major contractors involved in the ABM (anti-ballistic missile) system—a formidable lobby indeed.

Contracts are written to be as risk free as possible for corporations, with government bearing the burden of cost overruns, of design deficiencies, and often furnishing plant and equipment. The defense market is made secure and stable, negotiated rather than competitive bidding is too often the practice, and profits are allowed which are frequently far out of proportion to the minimal risks incurred.

When the government changes its mind about a contractor, it pays cancellation penalties. When a project goes sour, the contractor is given fees so he can keep his "management team intact." When, through gross mismanagement, a firm gets in trouble, the government bails it out. And when the whole aerospace industry feels a financial pinch, a new round of weapons is the government's response.

Although the avowed public policy favors competition, the structure of the defense sector involves practices such as "weapon system managers," subcontracting, and "single source procurement" which foster collusion and concentration and do away with the self-correcting market mechanism. It is ironic that an industry whose purpose is supposedly to defend the free enterprise system is one in which competition is the exception (only 12% of Pentagon procurement for FY 1971 was made through open, competitive bidding).

In 1971, an independent analysis by the General Accounting Office of $4.3 billion worth of defense business found the average rate of return on investment to be 56%. Yet in the face of this, the Secretary of Defense announced that new procurement policies would allow even higher profits in the future. The government and military practices of privatization in the Iraq War have put those historic figures to shame. The shipping of 20 tons of hundred-dollar bills for personal distribution by the occupying power gives you some idea of the level of fiscal depravity to which government leaders have fallen.

In 1946, the first secretary of defense, James Forrestal, told the graduating class of the Armed Forces Information School, "It is your responsibility to make citizens aware of their responsibility to the services." Every element of American society is marshaled to support the warfare state. Everyone loves a parade and the military goes all out to show its stuff before the home folk. Armed Forces Day ceremonies throughout the land typically draw large crowds to nearby military bases (and surprising numbers of them are nearby). Children are especially welcome, for it is important that the image-making begin early in shaping a favorable view of the military. Community leaders are placed on advisory panels of various sorts, flown to firepower demonstrations, and hosted at military installations. Even though military men are supposed to execute policy, not make it or propagandize for it, teams of officers conduct indoctrination seminars on world affairs and national security, frequently sponsored by the local chamber of commerce.

The Department of Defense budgets lobbying efforts and indoctrination of the public under the guise of information programs. Yet it is outraged when a solitary television documentary attempts to expose the peddling of the Pentagon. Defense contractors spend huge sums (reimbursed, of course, as a "normal business expense") on the glorification of airplanes, missiles, ships and guns.

All of the propaganda has created a great reservoir of favorable support, which has paid off handsomely for the military and its industrial associates by providing a barrier to criticism that is hard to penetrate. However bad the product or mismanaged the weapons program, no major contractor is really called to account for failures.

It is important that citizens resist the military line. When the Pentagon sends speakers or propaganda films are shown in local communities, citizens should protest the showings and arrange to present speakers and documentaries portraying the true dimensions of American militarism and questioning the accuracy of the information fed to them by the Pentagon. Outside experts and informed citizens can be invited to speak to local clubs and citizen groups. Regional conferences can be organized, bringing together experts and citizens to explore the issues of foreign policy and defense. The American people must be made to realize that they are continuously victims of a bald misrepresentation about the threats we face and the defense we need.

NIKITA KHRUSHCHEV tells in his memoirs of a conversation he had with President Eisenhower at Camp David. The President asked him how he decided on funds for military expenses, but then added, "Perhaps first I should tell you how it is with us... My military leaders say, 'Mr. President, we need such and such a sum for such and such a program.' I say, 'Sorry, we don't have the funds.' They say, 'We have reliable information that the Soviet Union has already allocated funds for their own such program.' So I give in... Now tell me, how is it with you?"

And Khrushchev replied, "It's just the same. Some people say, 'Comrade Khrushchev, look at this! The Americans are developing such and such a system.' I tell them there's no money. So we discuss it some more, and I end up by giving them the money they ask for."

The same race is ever present. Political leadership seems incapable of resisting the persistent pressures from the military-industrial complex for ever-advancing weapons technologies. In the absence of such independent political judgments, military procurement comes to be determined by inter-service and interagency competition, aided and abetted by the two largest private constituencies in our society, the business-corporate constituency and labor, augmented by the patriotic feelings of the people which all military leaders call upon at budget time.

President Nixon admitted, in his first administration, that "we and our NATO allies do not believe that war is imminent in Europe," but, he asserted, "we must face the possibility that it could occur." Of course, war could occur; but the sane leader prepares for the most likely and realistic contingencies. It is time we re-examine whether or not we have become the victims of unreasonable paranoia. Are we wasting our treasure and depleting our domestic society in preparing for a war which the other side is not, and never has been, planning?

Have we, in fact, been increasing the chances of such a war through the rising level of armaments and the increasing tension, hostility, and chance of miscalculation which can in themselves be the cause of a war which no one wants? Because of the vivid memory of World War II and the terrorist attack of 9-11, we have maintained a high level of armaments in order to deter the aggression that might come if we were unprepared. Perhaps we should recall instead the situation which brought on World War I, when nations faced each other armed to the teeth, none wanting war, but each fearful of attack, until the war erupted out of the mutual fears the arms race had created.

Furthermore, in this nuclear era, no level of defense spending can guarantee security against attack. We can never hope to prevent truly staggering losses to our country in a nuclear war, regardless of the level of arms we maintain. *Our only hope of survival is to prevent the outbreak of war*, and this can be achieved in less expensive and more effective ways than by continuously building up our weapons arsenal. Through wise negotiations, through sensitive attention to the fears of other nations, through personal contacts at the governmental and private levels, and through the good offices of international organizations, we can strengthen the barriers to war.

Our national foreign policy has been just the opposite. Since the present Bush Administration has characterized terrorism as a "war" rather then a "criminal" act, it has established war as the permanent state of our foreign and domestic posture. It is no coincidence that this permanently strengthens the military-industrial complex.

Relying on Congress to bring sanity to defense funding is truly a fool's errand. The Pentagon is an entrenched bureaucracy and the defense industry essentially owns the government lock, stock, and barrel. If nothing else, since World War II, the Congress has shown itself incapable of bringing about change.

While it may be that lay citizens cannot judge the technical efficacy of particular weapons systems, they are quite capable of judging whether or not the United States should exercise its military muscle throughout the world. If the military budget were presented to them in terms which made clear its relation to foreign policy goals, and if much more information were made available, citizens would then be equipped to exercise overall political and civilian control of our military spending. But citizens lack the power, that of lawmaking, to exercise such control.

There is inadequate public supervision today of the appropriations process when defense spending is involved. There is an unwillingness to question defense expenditures (compared to the way domestic expenditures are scrutinized). There is a tendency to accept the recommendations of the military without questioning the reasoning behind their recommendations or the motivations which might have led to them. The military is assumed to have only the best interests of the country at heart and, beyond that, to have special expertise which qualifies it to make recommendations which mere civilians can question only from ignorance.

In considering motivations, we often fail to recognize that the military man behind his desk is like any other man, subject to the same kinds of bureaucratic pressures and to the tendency to identify his special interests with the general welfare. People easily come to believe that what is good for them is good for their country, and military men are not immune to this self-serving perspective. We must, then, question the opinions of persons in the military just as much as we question the opinions of businessmen. Each is concerned for his country, but each may develop narrow viewpoints which blind him to broader picture of our national interest.

I must emphasize that I do not mean to disparage our military, either their courage on the battlefield or their dedication to the country. They serve to the best of their ability both on the battlefield and behind a desk. But, we have seen too many instances in history, culminating in the catastrophe of Vietnam and now Iraq and potentially in Iran, where the abdication of responsibility by the Congress and the concentration of military power in the president/commander-in-chief has led to disaster. I, for one, fear the expansion of this power with nuclear weapons and all that modern technology can make available far more than I fear the effects of imposing democratic constraints upon the president.

Now it is time for the voice of the people to be heard, demanding that Congress again play its constitutional role as watchdog of the military and guardian of civilian control. Only the people can make Congress assert its judgment on the defense budget. History has shown that the people can't even do that absent legislative power equal to that of their legislative representatives.

IT IS GENERALLY AGREED that the underlying basis of our national security is the education and health level of our people and the strength of our national economy. This is our real line of defense.

Apologists for the military argue that massive defense spending is a boon to the U.S. economy. This is false. Although the direct beneficiaries of military spending form a powerful constituency in favor of it, the U.S. economy as a whole would be far healthier with a much smaller defense budget. The substitution of other types of expenditures, i.e., research and development of alternative energy sources, rebuilding our nation's infrastructure, would over a relatively short period create much more income and employment than would be lost through cutbacks in military spending. Protection money, whether paid to Old Chicago mobsters or modern America's defense contractors, benefits no one but the "protector" whose pocket gets lined.

There would be problems associated with a shift away from defense spending. Some workers would be laid off, and particular regions of the country could be hard hit. There would be rapid depreciation of specialized skills and equipment. There might be some temporary falling off of total demand and economic momentum, but the real pain for individuals could be eased by compensatory measures or even eliminated by the adoption of imaginative transitional programs like maintaining all employees displaced at 80% of their salaries until they are retrained and rehired in some new capacity. After WW II the massive industrial capabilities of the nation were readily reoriented to produce for the peacetime domestic comforts in what became "the Golden Age" of America.

After the initial dislocations, I believe we would have a far healthier economy. The funds released from the military budget could be used to finance the rebuilding of our cities, the provision of decent housing for all our citizens, cleaning up of our environment, and to finance the many other improvements to our financially starved "infrastructure." Past experience supports the notion that our economy will grow more rapidly with a higher proportion of domestic spending. This was the case after World War II, the Korean War and the Vietnam War as the economy rather painlessly converted to peacetime production.

A special issue is the probable impact of defense cutbacks on the research and development industry. The Department of Defense finances more than half the R & D performed in high-technology industries, such as aircraft, electrical and communications equipment.

So, as an occupational group, scientists and engineers will suffer proportionately greater job dislocation than any other group, when military spending is cut. However, this talent would then be open to entrepreneurial adventures which we see leading our technical advancement in the world today.

The initiatives that I have suggested in Chapter 6, to deal with the environment and energy crises have the potential to use all of the scientific and technical resources that we and our global partners can muster. As one example, the October 10, 2007 report by the National Security Space Office on Space-Based Solar Power (SBSP), points to a solution. An accelerated effort to develop space-based solar power would require scientists and engineers with similar skills to the ones currently used for developing military systems—computers, rockets, sensors, advanced materials, etc. This report suggests that SBSP development can result in delivery of carbon-free electrical energy at costs competitive to coal. Full development of SBSP would require the mining of the Moon and very advanced technology with a purpose not for military domination but to reduce the dependence of our country and the world on oil. This would fulfill national security requirements while at the same time combating global warming.

IN BRINGING ABOUT MILITARY CUTBACKS, we can expect resistance from communities that would be hit hard by reductions. There would be understandable concern about the impact on local economies through the loss of jobs; this is a legitimate worry when a military base or defense contractor is the town's main industry. We must provide assistance in the form of financial aid and relocation of new industries to these communities to help them through their readjustment period. In doing this, we should remember that the military holds an enormous amount of valuable real estate that could be converted to recreational use, to industrial parks, schools, and to home-building sites. Intelligently redeveloped, these installations could become the nucleus for a rejuvenation of many towns and cities on a solid peacetime economy.

A great deal of military restructuring and the closing of some 700 military bases overseas can be used to strengthen and expand bases within the continental United States. We have a military presence in over 130 countries. We have become the policeman of the world in order to sustain a rationale for a military-industrial complex. This may feed the hubris of our leaders, but does little for the well-being of the average American.

In sum, there are ways to bring the runaway warfare state under control. Many have already tried to do it, but military hawks have managed to call into question their patriotism and discredit them as insufficiently aware of the threat our way of life faces. These war mongers have drugged America with fear for the last 50 years. The culture has been militarized and apathetic to the dangers domestically and internationally of American imperialism. We must persist in our call for a return to reason until the people see clearly what we have become as a nation, and say, "Enough is enough!"

Most of the preceding text in this chapter, except for references to the Iraq War and events of today, was written in 1971. Needless to say, the description of the military-industrial complex and the level of military appropriations at the height of the Vietnam War pale by comparison to the mess we find ourselves in today with the Iraq War and our imperialistic global leadership. I purposely repeat the optimistic solution I had at the time: "Now it is time for the voice of the people to be heard, demanding that Congress again play its constitutional role as watchdog of the military and guardian of civilian control. Only the people can make the Congress assert its judgment on the defense budget."

It is disheartening to revisit my optimism then, only to realize that in the ensuing 37 years, the problems I recounted then have grown considerably worse. I left office in 1981, discouraged by Congress's inability to address this vital subject and so many others that cry out for attention. The futility of appealing to the people to control the Congress underscored my naïveté at the time. Our electoral process does not begin to invest the people with the necessary power to control Congress.

The optimistic view I held then is the view most Americans hold today: elect good people to Congress and everything will be righted. Tragically, representative government does not operate that way; nevertheless, media pundits perpetuate the myth that the people, without the central power of government—the power to make laws— can control public policy.

> We are all about to lose a country—ours, not Iraq. The greatest casualty of this war is the image we have of ourselves and the reality of what we have become. How did matters get to this point? How have we moved from Norman Rockwell's America to a United States where violence, torture, mendaciousness, spying, propaganda, and disregard for the law have become the new patriotism?
>
> *Senator Lowell Weicker, 2007*

[On a note of interest: Lowell served with me in the Senate and was the ranking member on the Building and Grounds subcommittee that I chaired and used to release the *Pentagon Papers* into the public record. As punishment for what I did, the Environment and Public Works Committee required that I personally pay the subcommittee's publication cost of the *Pentagon Papers*—approximately $400. Lowell insisted on paying half the cost.]

To demonstrate the full extent of our misguided military spending, I extracted information on the 2008 defense budget from Winslow T. Wheeler's *"Ringing Up the Bill for America's Defense"* published March 4, 2007 in the Fort Worth Star-Telegram and by the McClatchy-Tribune News Service. Mr. Wheeler is a former Defense Department official who has published extensively on Pentagon matters and is now director of the Straus Military Reform Project with the Center for Defense Information.

According to Mr. Wheeler, President Bush requested a Pentagon budget for fiscal 2008 of $481 billion. To determine total U.S. security costs, however, add $142 billion to cover the anticipated costs of the wars in Iraq and Afghanistan and a supplemental in excess of $40 billion; add $17 billion requested for nuclear weapons costs in the Department of Energy; add another $5 billion for miscellaneous defense costs in other agencies, such as the General Services Administration's National Defense Stockpile, the Selective Service, and some Coast Guard and international FBI costs; and you get a grand total of $687 billion for 2008.

However, an inclusive definition of our defense budget might also include homeland security costs; for those expenses (beyond the ones already in the Defense Department), add $36 billion. In addition, there are other essential U.S. security costs in the budget of the State Department for diplomacy, arms aid to allies, U.N. peacekeeping, reconstruction aid for Iraq and Afghanistan, and foreign aid for other countries; add all or most of the International Affairs budget ($38 billion).

Add another $84 billion for the Department of Veterans Affairs, the human costs of past and current wars. Add another $75 billion, the share of annual payments on the interest of the national debt that can be attributed to the Defense Department. There's more—various defense-related costs, such as costs to the Treasury for military retirement, are distributed all over the federal government. The total for costs identified here come to $920 billion for 2008, a huge amount, but there will probably be even more.

For many years, the Congressional Budget Office (CBO) has found that the Defense Department underestimates its own costs to develop, produce, and maintain weapons and to support military personnel—beyond the other underestimations of war costs. If the CBO is right (and just about every Pentagon budget analyst says it is), add somewhere between $50 billion and $100 billion, just for 2008.

The actual total for 2008 is unknown; but it will be more than the $920 billion cited above. Spending just for Pentagon expenses in 2008 is today larger in inflation-adjusted dollars than at any point since the end of World War II. If truth be told, the Defense Department by its own admission is un-auditable and has been that way for decades. The Department of Homeland Security has now just joined its ranks as another budgetary sinkhole.

According to the International Institute for Strategic Studies in London, the rest of the world spent just over $611 billion on defense in 2005, the latest year available. That compares to the $510 billion we spent on just Pentagon costs that year. And with most foreign defense budgets stagnant or shrinking and ours growing rapidly, we can be confident that the United States now exceeds the rest of the world combined in defense spending.

According to the CIA's World Fact Book, the next biggest defense spender in the world, China, spent $81 billion in 2005—a very poor second place; it's just 13% of the $625 billion that our Pentagon will spend directly in 2008.

A study by the Swedish Institute places the U.S. at 46% of the world's total for defense expenditures, with Britain and France at 5% each, and Japan at 4%. China was placed at 4% and Russia at 3%.

The Democrats now in control of Congress made multiple promises to restore oversight of the war in Iraq and the executive branch in general; they are either being conned by the White House, the military services and the war-profiteering defense contractors or they are complicit in allowing the war machine to continue to dominate our federal budget and sustain American Imperialism. Do we need this level of military expenditures to defend ourselves—from whom? Whom do we fear?

Who will pay the bill? The price of American imperialism will be very clear to our grandchildren.

The Democrats in Congress are unlikely to make any tough choices. Neither will the Republicans. None will dare share with the public that America is bankrupt to the tune of a $50 trillion fiscal gap.

How can we all change direction? Two things need to happen. First, we need to elect a president who has the courage, desire and skill to bring the military-industrial complex to heel. And second, the people need to be empowered to make laws by enacting the National Initiative (see Chapter 2). The people could then reverse American Imperialism and end their role as the world's policeman.

America's Triumphal Imperialism

We're Number One in the:

>Production of military weaponry;
>
>Export of military weaponry;
>
>Number of deliverable nuclear warheads;
>
>Sale of nuclear power plants, all of which can produce the feed stock for nuclear weapons;
>
>Arms race in space;
>
>Number of countries where we station our military;
>
>Number of mercenary soldiers we employ;
>
>Consumer spending;
>
>Public, corporate and personal debt;
>
>Amount of indebtedness to other countries;
>
>Number of people we have in jail;
>
>Amount of pollution we produce;
>
>Amount of carbon energy we consume;
>
>War we wage on drugs; and
>
>Delusion and hubris that sustains American imperialism.

11

Global Governance

*More than an end to war, we want
an end to the beginnings of all wars—yes, an
end to this brutal, inhuman and thoroughly
impractical method of settling the differences
between governments.*
President Franklin D. Roosevelt

THE AMERICAN PEOPLE are experiencing a profound loss of faith in their nation's purposes in the world, and the world has lost respect for America's leadership. They see their leaders unable to deal effectively with the problems that face the nation, either domestically or on the foreign scene. They realize that their government is unable to protect its people from harm; it cannot promote economic development, either overseas in underdeveloped nations or in the underdeveloped inner cities of our own country; and it cannot work its military will on small but stubborn countries halfway around the world—or 90 miles off our shore. Many Americans are asking if our institutions and leaders are capable of responding to the contemporary world's social, moral and economic issues.

In the eyes of the rest of the world, our country has shown itself to be not as it likes to view itself, the preserver of world order, the exemplar of freedom and democracy, but as a belligerent country disrupting world order. Our pattern of using our immense power—both economic and military—where and when we please has made us the world's most dangerous nation. I am not saying that other nations are necessarily more peace-loving than we or that they are less willing than we to use force to achieve their goals. It is only that we have the power to be a danger to world peace, with no constraints on our nation's leaders but their own moral judgment—and we have learned in Vietnam and now in Iraq to our horror how shockingly lacking our leaders are in moral judgment.

Our actions in Iraq have created threats to our own security, making us our own worst enemy. We are paying dearly for our blunders, not only in loss of life, but in loss of faith in government. This is the ultimate threat to a nation, when people no longer have confidence in government.

America has a long anti-colonial tradition, going back to its beginnings. The recognition that we have become an imperial power has not been a pleasant one for Americans, and we shield ourselves from it by pretending that our kind of empire is somehow different from those that preceded us. It is true that we do not want to colonize the land ourselves, but we want to determine the type of government the people may have. We want them to join us in military alliance and permit us to base our armed forces and intelligence services on their soil, and we want the right to invest in, and thus to exploit, their natural resources. We are playing exactly the same role in the underdeveloped world as the British, the French, the Dutch, and the Germans did before us. We are pursuing in Iraq a colonial policy—control of their oil—through military occupation in a post-colonial world.

Out of the caldrons of Vietnam and Iraq we have learned that our innocent dream of being a benevolent empire is destined to be, in the end, no more benevolent than the cruel empires of yore. We cannot mold societies so different from our own to our liking, but must allow them to develop in their own way.

We must let them work out their own destiny, true to the character of their own diverse cultures. Our attempts to "modernize" them, that is to mold them in our image, by force if necessary, inflict far more destruction on these societies, than they would ever inflict themselves, if left to their own, less "modern" devices.

The global crisis brought on by nuclear weapons, assaults on the environment, population growth, and the advance of technology demands from us higher standards of humanity and wisdom than ever before. But the nation-state has shown itself unable to respond to this challenge. America is the most powerful example; but it is not alone in its inability to respond to the needs of this era. While people everywhere are searching for a style of life and a set of institutions which will promote humane life, the expansionist interest of many nation-states continue to pursue the course of death and to use their most advanced talents to magnify still further their ability to inflict oppression on already-suffering populations.

WE HAVE WITNESSED in the United States during the past quarter century a growing separation of the state apparatus, including the presidency, the Department of Defense, the CIA, FBI, the Department of State, and associated agencies, from the people it is supposed to be protecting. It is axiomatic that the custodians of the state will attempt to preserve it and to advance its interests. But when the state surrounds itself with the structures of secrecy, creates a loyalty system to ensure that those who serve it possess its values, and maintains a surveillance network to detect and apprehend citizens who oppose its purposes, then we are far along toward a 1984-style state system which suppresses its citizens to serve its own interests first and foremost.

In such a state system, policy makers act on the international scene to advance their own interests and those of the state, rather than those of the citizens they are supposed to represent or the people in other lands affected by their policies. In Vietnam, Laos, Cambodia, and Iraq we have seen our leaders decimate whole countries and destroy the societies of those countries, simply to preserve their own reputations for toughness and determination.

In the United States, our leaders have wanted to keep America first, even though that meant maintaining the world's largest arsenal of destruction: we would be first in death, even if we could not be first in life in healthcare, in quality of education, in concern for the aged and the underprivileged, in support for culture, and in all the activities that make life worth living.

While we begin to recognize our limitations, both of understanding and resources, we must gain the confidence to relate to other nations on the same basis as lesser powers have for centuries—using negotiation, peaceful contacts, and trade, expecting to win some contests and lose others, but retaining a belief in our ability to participate productively on the world scene in a peaceful and cooperative fashion.

Many factors point to a new era in world relations. Europe, both East and West, is demonstrating renewed self confidence and vitality, suggesting the ability to determine its own defense needs and to meet them through its own, not inconsiderable resources, based on its own perceptions of the threats it faces. Western Europe's GNP is fully 80% of our own, and it is quite capable of meeting its own defense requirements.

IN DEALING WITH THE UNDEVELOPED WORLD, we must recognize that most of the existing governments are composed of conservative elites which hold onto their positions of power and privilege by force of arms (usually purchased from the United States). If all the people of these nations are to benefit from modernization there will likely be revolutionary struggles in which political control is wrested from the traditional ruling classes and a program of land reform, education, and economic reform having mass support is instituted. The United States may want to resist these developments, but the pressures from the unhappy masses are overwhelming. In the end we will find ourselves shut out of these countries entirely, if we do not alter our view of what constitutes beneficial changes in these lands.

We must recognize that there are real limits to how much we can influence another country. Foreign affairs analyst and author of *The Politics of Hysteria*, William Pfaff has wisely written that "foreign policy is fundamentally a means by which the American nation is protected, and it is not an appropriate vehicle for reform or revolution of foreign societies." We need only reflect on our inability to solve the problems we have within our own country to recognize the far greater limitations we have when we attempt to introduce change in other nations. Nor should our military power be applied to enforce our will. With the rise of sophisticated techniques of guerrilla warfare and new means of communicating ideas—and hence of arousing latent national feelings and welding popular movements together—great powers, regardless of the military force they deploy, should no longer exert control over territory not occupied by their own citizens.

Our country should not attempt to take on the tasks of the United Nations or manage political and economic change around the world, or be the police force of the world. We can only assist, with our extraordinary wealth and industrial capacity, as young countries attempt to find their own ways toward a better life. We must become, again, the champion of revolutionary change and of decolonization, leading the world in new norms of international law, appropriate to an age of economic interdependence.

Just as we believe in the supremacy of law over might in relations within our nation, we must begin to apply these same standards in our dealings with other nations. I believe that only when we recognize this and begin to take international institutions seriously will we at last be on the road to workable arrangements for preserving the peace. Our world leadership should be exercised, not through might as in the past, but through moral example, economic aid, and support for international law and institutions.

Equally, our subversive activities must be curtailed in order that our presence can be a legitimate one and that the small entanglements that lead to big wars can be avoided. The CIA and our other intelligence agencies serve as a direct arm of our interventionist policy, providing the information on which military preparations are based, subverting revolutionary governments, and, at times, organizing and leading covert armies. We need to know something about potential adversaries, but essential information can be provided today by reconnaissance satellites and by reading published information.

The clandestine activities in which our government engages today do not truly defend our nation. They serve only to allow the executive branch to project itself overseas. They create and preserve client regimes. They overthrow obstreperous regimes that refuse to kowtow to America. They advance American business interests by bribing friendly government officials and defaming the opposition. Finally, they engage in the kind of improper and, at times, illegal activities which most Americans would object to if any country but their own were engaged in them.

In pursuing what our leaders have deemed to be our "national interest," we have too often flouted international law and prior international agreements and, by this action, reduced the effectiveness of these restraints for maintaining world peace. A policy of pursuing "vital interest" above all is a policy of "beggar thy neighbor." Such a policy by the most powerful nation on Earth guarantees that the nations of the world will remain in beggary.

THE COMPLEXITY AND REMOTENESS of international affairs seem to suggest that effective citizen action is impossible. On many issues an informed portion of our citizens already has at least as good a grasp on foreign affairs as their elected representatives in Congress. For instance, every year thousands of Americans travel abroad and get a clearer mental picture of the world. A picture is worth a thousand words. A visit is a million pictures. Citizens are no less capable of making informed decisions on the monumental questions of foreign policy issues than their leaders.

How can the lone citizen have an influence on these issues? It isn't as hard as it sometimes seems. First, he should see that he and other members of his community are informed. Local organizations such as world affairs councils, UN support groups, World Federalist chapters are effective venues for information and discussion.

Our policy should be to strengthen the institutions of cooperation and conventions of international law. We must seize upon every opportunity to press for cooperation and the peaceful means of settling all disputes.

Looking back 37 years, the best and the brightest of the liberal and moderate leadership were the ones that brought us into the quagmire of Vietnam. We have a replay with the best and brightest of moderate Republicans and far-right religious conservatives taking us into Iraq. What's more immoral today is that at least we could say we were in Vietnam for fear of communism but in fact there was more than a passing interest in the rubber and other resources of that country. Now, it's all about oil. There was a fear of communism back then, but today In Iraq we don't even have that to offer. Arguments were made in fear of terrorism but that was not the case. Iraq under Saddam Hussein posed no threat to the United States and, in fact, no weapons of mass destruction were ever found there.

What was apparent with the Vietnam experience, and now with the Iraq experience is the chasm of distrust that exists between the people and their government. This chasm now is being maintained through the wanton use of secrecy by the government. Since *Citizen Power* was first written, we have seen the implosion of communism, the realization of freedom in the Warsaw Pact countries, the opening up of Chinese and Russian market economies, China maintaining itself as a communist country, and Russia becoming a capitalist democracy. Vietnam has now become a most favored nation trading partner of the United States. You can buy a Baskin Robbins ice cream cone or Kentucky Fried Chicken in Hanoi, and yet our vindictiveness over Vietnam not permitting us to "win" (whatever *that* means) resulted in our mean-spirited punishment of the Vietnamese with sanctions for a generation.

In terms of foreign policy, fear mongering has persisted more subtly than we choose to admit, from the fear of communism to the fear of Islamism, and the fear of "Jihadism." The whole attitude of fear drills right down through the national psyche with the fear of blacks, Latinos, Chinese, gays, the fear of women asserting their power, and a whole host of other fears. It is just a jumble of fear that translates into foreign policy that is an aberration where we define our public interest as always superior to the public interest of the rest of the world. That kind of a definition leaves very little room for accommodation between peoples and nations. We act as if the "American dream" is the only dream that is valid; as if other nations don't have a right to their own dream.

As a result, it brought us to the point with Vietnam where we were not able to admit our error. We refused to accept the fact that we made a grievous mistake in Vietnam and that our troops died in vain and that over three million Vietnamese and Southeast Asians died in vain at our hands.

When we make a mistake and refuse to admit it, we likely will repeat the mistake; certainly a sign of immaturity in our personal lives. We develop maturity by acknowledging our mistakes and making the necessary correction to avoid repeating them in the future; that's how we permit our children to improve, by acknowledging and learning from their mistakes.

When we failed to admit the mistake of Vietnam, we set ourselves up to repeat that mistake in Iraq.

World War II brought to us advances in science that gave human beings the capacity to destroy the planet with a single global nuclear exchange. Science has given us the ability to destroy the planet, which we are in the process of doing over time as a result of industrialization's impact on the environment. Essentially, what we are doing through our use of energy, our despoliation of the environment is literally cooking ourselves off the planet, quite possibly within a hundred years. This dilemma of human economic outreach organized by corporate society is part of the process that we call globalization.

This process is lowering the national barriers that all countries guard jealousy under the name of sovereignty, and they are being lowered in a pell mell, unorganized fashion that, as a result, will cause a great deal of suffering, because corporations essentially have no morality, memory or sense of responsibility to future generations. They are motivated by profit. And so greed and profit become the operative agents of globalization. We try with new institutions and trade agreements to regulate globalization but fail at the altar of profit. The state-less economic organizations of globalization are operating in regulatory no-man's land.

These three elements threatening the planet—nuclear annihilation, environmental extinction, and the anarchy of globalization—need not be the norm for human existence. The tragedy is that the planet has sufficient resources to satisfy the needs of all human beings if we had the capacity to manage them. That brings us to the need for a United Nations that can govern the global community.

It is unfortunate that at the close of the Age of Enlightenment, human governance topped out at the nation-state level, rather than progressing to the global level. The nation-state holds itself sovereign. At the last effort at global governance, after the Second World War, the victors enshrined their power in a Security Council with veto powers; thereby holding hostage the public interest of all other people in the world to their selfish foreign policy interests.

The answer at this point takes us back to Chapter 2, which points to the methodology for arriving at a system of equitable global governance. At heart, it is the issue of sovereignty—something a human being acquires at birth. The individual is sovereign.

People attach their sovereignty to their particular nation-state to the point of jingoistic idiocy. The same emotions that we attach to athletics are superimposed in an exaggerated fashion on the nation-state. As lives are lost in riots after athletic events, so too are many more lives lost in the irrational fervor of competing nation-states. This excessive patriotism for one's own nation becomes the worst form of mob action.

The sovereign individual citizen cedes a certain degree of sovereignty at every level of government, whether it is at the local level, the state level, or national. The individual has no sovereignty left except for the brief moments when he or she exercises it on Election Day. I am suggesting that we shift a degree of sovereignty, already lost to the individual at the federal level (nation-state), to a global institution for some degree of governance in the no-man's land of world anarchy.

The present, inadequate system of global governance fractures sovereignty, not unlike what existed at the founding of our country before the sovereign colonies were united in a federal system of United States. How do we repair those fractures? It starts with the process of empowering the people in one country at a time, something that has started in Switzerland in 1848 and has ripened with great success; and yet the Swiss model has not been sufficiently appreciated by the people of the world to incite its widespread emulation. If the United States were successful in bringing about the federal ballot initiative, the National Initiative for Democracy where the people are empowered as lawmakers, this advance would race around the world like wildfire and set the stage to restructure the United Nations.

The next step to expand the National Initiative would be to seek enactment in the Organization for Economic Co-operation and Development countries (OECD), plus India, China, and Brazil. Once people in those countries are empowered to share power with their elected government officials, the people of the world could call for a convention under the auspices of the United Nations, and then restructure the United Nations to do away with the veto power of the Security Council.

A Council of Regions could replace the Security Council. It would be divided into geographic regions like the European Union, South American, North American, Southeast Asia and the Middle East. China and India are sufficiently populous to be entities unto themselves.

The restructuring of the UN General Assembly would be based upon population and quality of governance within each nation. Let's say China is a member, but does not have a complete democratic structure of governance, it would not enjoy the full weight of delegates to reflect its population. Sweden, Finland and other Scandinavian countries because of their unusual level of successful democratic governance would have their number of delegates weighted to reflect the success of governance at home. The weighted formula would take into consideration the political, social and economic performance of each nation-state.

We need not worry about the tyrannies of the world or the countries which are not mature enough to move to this level of governance. If the OECD countries and key countries like India, China, Brazil, the United States, Russia, and the European Union come into this system, no country would choose to be left out. They would all clamor to get in, and like the European Union, they would have to adhere to a certain standard of human governance; that standard would require in the minimum that the people be empowered as lawmakers in their country.

In summary, what we're talking about is that the source of sovereignty at all levels of government is the sovereignty of individuals.

Dwight Eisenhower said, "I like to believe that people in the long run are going to do more to promote peace than our governments. Indeed, I think that people want peace so much that one of these days, governments had better get out of the way and let them have it."

The National Initiative is the vehicle to accomplish a restructuring of the global polity for world governance and bring about peace and equitable management of the Earth's resources for the benefit of its peoples.

Global Governance

Americans must recognize we have wandered far from our intended national purpose and world leadership role.`

Failures in Vietnam and Iraq have taught us that we have lost our moral compass, departing dramatically from America's long anti-colonial tradition.

The gulf between the government and the people has grown ever greater, furthered largely by pervasive secrecy structures.

We have established priorities that advance state interests internationally rather than addressing citizen concerns at home.

We must abandon notions of forcing other peoples to accept our ways and instead reframe our views of what constitutes beneficial changes in undeveloped nations.

For our own national security, we must curtail subversive intrusions and clandestine activities abroad.

We need to lead the world in new standards of international law through moral example, economic aid, and support for international law and institutions.

To grow into civic maturity, we must admit our mistakes and learn from them to avoid repetition.

By empowering people at home, we would advance the idea of direct democracy abroad and, in so doing, restructure the United Nations to become a global institution of governance that recognizes individual sovereignty.

The National Initiative can restructure the global polity for world governance and, at the same time, enjoy peace and equitably share the Earth's resources with all peoples.

12

Who Stole the American Dream?

The present state of things is the
consequence of the past;
and it is natural to inquire as to
the sources of the good we enjoy
or the evils we suffer.
Samuel Johnson

The title of this chapter is the same as it was 37 years ago. I thought of freedom, and personal and civil liberty, as uniquely American. I think most of us believe this without realizing that such national hubris devalues the concept.

The dream of freedom, respect for individual sovereignty, is not uniquely American; it began with civilization. The struggle to prevent enslavement or subjugation in any relationship is universal in all people.

The title of this chapter suggests that some force has been denying us our dream while, at the same time, bombarding us with jingoistic rhetoric that the American dream is the pinnacle of human achievement. My present analysis is somewhat better informed by the intervening years from the beginning of my Senate career when the book was first published in 1972 to the present. My view of the corporation—an institution lacking memory and morality—is not less harsh; however, my view of government—a tool for cooperative action—has become harsher.

All of our efforts at improving public policy are rooted in the structure of representative government. Unfortunately, we continue to believe that electing the right people to public office will bring about beneficial change. So we repeat over and over again something that has been proven repeatedly not to work. I do not diminish the vital need to elect people of integrity to public office. The point I make is that such elections are not nearly enough to overcome the shortcomings of representative government.

ALL PEOPLES DREAM of freedom and happiness, particularly those who have experienced the inequities and repressions of autocratic governments. We Americans were blessed with the opportunity to realize our dream of freedom at the confluence of the Scottish, English, and French Ages of Enlightenment in the 18th Century, when ancient Greek concepts of democracy experienced a rebirth. Nevertheless, we had to struggle for our freedom with blood and sacrifice in a revolutionary war. It wasn't until 1787 that the structure of our government took permanent shape, the design of which became a beacon that would guide the peoples of the world toward a system of representative government.

When the Constitutional Framers met in Philadelphia, their options in designing our new government were unduly influenced by the fact that the 13 confederate states, all independently sovereign, were in the process of falling apart internally and as a confederation. The convention delegates were the wealthy elites of those states; any loss of civic cohesion would directly affect their personal property. Their initial preference for the structure of a new government, derived from the successful colonial experience with the town meeting system of governance, should have produced an amalgam of representative and direct citizen involvement in government.

Unfortunately, the pall of slavery gripped the convention's proceedings, holding hostage any possible truly democratic success.

Compounding the tragedy the Framers were about to initiate was the fact that probably the best opportunity to rid the nation of the scourge of slavery was the period from the cessation of the Revolutionary War hostilities in 1781 to the beginning of the Philadelphia Convention in May 1787. Free blacks and slaves had fought in the Revolutionary War in numbers that exceeded their demographic distribution and king cotton had yet to take command of the Deep South with Eli Whitney's gin. Blacks had earned their piece of the dream.

I believe the point at which the American dream of freedom was eclipsed was when the delegates to the convention failed to keep faith with the principles of the Declaration of Independence articulated 11 years earlier. That Declaration was the dream, the vision—all men are created equal. Delegate John Rutledge of South Carolina, backed by the delegates of Georgia, blackmailed James Madison, the architect of the convention, and the rest of the delegates into accepting slavery as the price for their states joining the new government.

The Framers compromised the moral principles articulated in the Declaration of Independence and made a deal with the devil in order to unify a new nation and prevent the certain collapse of the Confederate States that threatened their personal wealth and power. The legacy of slavery plagues us to this day. Repeated generational transfers of cruel, inhuman norms of conduct toward fellow humans, rationalized by Holy Scripture, have damaged the American psyche, beyond repair. We are a violent people, still sustained by religious fervor. And we wonder why.

The American psyche was further coarsened by the national sense of "manifest destiny," the idea that God wished us to exercise dominion over the land. Land represented economic freedom and a chance for upward mobility. The land of the continent was there for the taking, even though the land was already occupied by the Indians. In a cruel electoral calculus, settlers used their government's military power to legalize their continued encroachments on Indian lands. Settlers voted; Indians did not. The Indians were not enslaved but nearly annihilated.

The Constitutional Framers, the elites of their day, created a system of representative government that held a monopoly of legislative power that facilitated policies that shame us to this day. Regardless of how much we praise our form of government, it cannot by any stretch of the imagination be called egalitarian or democratic. Our Constitution, creating the structure of representative government, favors elites simply because it was written by elites. And, of course, they did not fail to provide for the continuity of their own power by establishing procedures whereby they could amend the Constitution with Article V and make laws with Article VII.

Our Constitution has been extensively copied around the world. Obviously, the structure of representative government does not threaten other elites governing foreign societies.

The Framers wrote a document that defined the first constitutional representative government in history. Representative government has since been the norm in all democracies except Switzerland, which copied our Constitution but added one very powerful change, which represents the next step in the evolution of democracy. The Swiss Constitution, written in 1848, added the people as lawmakers creating a very successful governing partnership with their elected officials. This was the intended road but the one not taken by the Framers of the American Constitution.

THE FRAMERS HAD TO EXCLUDE the people from the ratification process in order to secure the ratification of their flawed Constitution. They had a daunting task. They had to avoid a vote in the Confederate Congress, where the Constitution would likely not have been ratified. Similarly, they had to avoid votes in the state legislatures by persuading them to refer ratification to state conventions called for that purpose. The convention scenario also permitted the Framers to circumvent the people, denying them a legislative role in the ratification process.

In 1778, Massachusetts placed before its citizens a constitution for ratification that included slavery. The people refused to ratify it. In 1780, a constitution authored by John Adams that excluded slavery was then overwhelmingly ratified. The Framers in Philadelphia were well aware of ordinary people's attitude toward slavery, so they figured out how to keep them one step removed from the ratification process; that was to have the state legislatures call for state conventions and refer the Constitution for ratification to them. The elites then controlled the conventions. This had universal appeal. It offered a way to kill the Constitution without the existing governments being held accountable. It permitted the political elites for and against the Constitution to gather and duke it out without being pestered by the real people.

Even with the success of overcoming these barriers, it was literally a miracle that the Constitution was ratified at all. Fifteen votes strategically placed in three states would have meant defeat. Would a Constitution *sans* slavery have fared better? I think so. At least the Framers would have had the integrity to put the ratification before the people who, as the Preamble stated, "do ordain…" The real impact of the people being cut out of this legislative act was to alter the entire nature and the rule of citizens in American governance to this day.

All of the Founders and Framers believed that the people had every right to exercise their legislative sovereignty to make laws. They are quoted frequently, pointing out that future generations have an obligation to alter their governments and constitutions to suit their interests. They also pointed with pride to the seminal lawmaking act of the Declaration of Independence. Nevertheless, they sacrificed the people's lawmaking right to protect the ratification of their compact with the devil—slavery. They locked into the Constitution by excluding procedures that rightly belonged in Article VII for the people to amend the Constitution and make laws. Their fears that the people would remove slavery from the Constitution if so empowered were well founded. The first lobbying act of the first Congress was an assault on slavery by Pennsylvania Quakers led by Benjamin Franklin. It was successfully thwarted by James Madison and accepted as an understanding in Congress that the subject would never be addressed again.

Slavery was so effectively embedded in the Constitution that its removal, short of a civil war, was impossible. Of the five features locking slavery into the Constitution, only one—that of a slave being counted as three-fifths of a person for representative purposes in the U.S. House—had been removed by the Civil War. The other four highly undemocratic features of the Constitution have remained to work their mischief on us to this day, long after the demise of slavery. They are: 1) the Electoral College, 2) Article V, 3) the U.S. Senate, and 4) state control of federal elections.

The amending process described in Article V is so undemocratic that the chambers (House and Senate) of the 13 smallest states can stop any national reform—a population ratio considerably less than 10%. Little wonder why so few changes have been made to update the Constitution to meet the needs of the 21st Century since its ratification in 1788. Other than housekeeping, the only changes to the Constitution have been the expansion of the voting franchise. The property requirements were essentially removed at the state level prior to the Civil War. The expansion of the voting franchise to male blacks was the product of the Civil War Reconstruction amendments. The way was paved for a federal amendment to include women in 1920 as a result of repeated passage of initiative and referendum laws granting women the right to vote by state governments.

From my perspective, the most damaging legacy of slavery on the Constitution, other than the exclusion of the legitimate exercise of the people's legislative power, is the control of federal elections by state governments. By controlling who could get elected to federal office—president, Congress—states asserted real power many times superior to the federal power based in the Constitution. This issue is better understood as "states' rights." It has kept in contention the supremacy of the federal government. This treatise is too short to treat the havoc that this issue has wrought on the nation.

THE FIRST FUNDAMENTAL CHANGE in American governance since the founding took place at the turn of the last century without amending the Constitution. Starting in 1898 and up until the First World War, more than 20 states amended their constitutions to permit their citizens to initiate and enact laws and amend constitutions. The motivation for the Initiative, Referendum, and Recall (IRR) laws was the abusive corruption of government by the business community in the post-Civil War boom and the "robber baron" era.

The legislative role of the people with different laws from state to state has not been consistent. Additionally, citizen lawmaking has not been independent of representative government, which has sought to use its control to continually diminish the people's legislative role.

The problem of citizen participation in government applies not only to those states with initiative law, but also to all states and at all levels of government. It has never been easy for people to participate in the political process except under the direction and control of political parties that hold a monopoly over the electoral process.

No force in history is more oppressive than government. There is never a guarantee that successful governance in one era will be passed down in a straight line to subsequent generations. So many factors come into the chain of human events that nothing can be guaranteed, and malevolent forces are always at play.

In this book, I have attempted to identify a number of important policy issues that face our nation today. I have the advantage of having dealt with most of them more than a generation ago. I have had to face up to disappointments as I looked back on my experiences. I am disheartened to see that political and social issues have gotten worse in the past 37 years, and many of the solutions proposed today, in my opinion, will make matters even worse.

I blame the competitive, confrontational structure of the Congress and the legislative monopoly it holds at the federal level. The Constitution distributes congressional representation geographically where the economic, resource, and social special interests of each state and each district come into competitive confrontation for the limited wealth of the whole government. Add to this a committee system designed to compartmentalize the specialization and expertise of individual members who are ruled over by committee chairmen and ranking members who acquire control of legislative empires by a seniority system regardless of competence.

I have yet to touch upon where the real machinations of the legislative process take place and where the ultimate control of government resides—in the political parties. They are not even referred to in the Constitution, and the Founders universally disdained them as odious "factions;" yet, they appeared in the first presidential administration of George Washington and to this day carry more clout than any power defined by the Constitution. Historically, they evolved around regional economic ideologies into a two-party monopoly, which they jealously guard with the full force of the law and the police power of government. It is to this unsanctioned power that gravitate the special interests of the nation who seek to influence the direction of public policy in a venue hidden from public view.

THE ABOVE DESCRIPTION of representative government is not meant to be pejorative in any way. It's how I experienced and understand the process. I do not believe those within representative government can correct it. There are only two venues for change—the government and the people; the solution is obvious. People must be brought into the governing process in the only possible role, that of lawmaker. I do not mean to imply that the people as individuals are superior in intellect to their leaders as individuals. Not at all. But the people acting as a constituency of the whole, legislating by majority rule, do not have barriers in making decisions involving the public interest. The constituent majority identifies and votes its enlightened self interest. That is not the case with representatives in government who have generic barriers in dealing with the public interest that in many cases do not coincide with their personal self interest, the financial interests of their backers or the interests of their political party in gaining or retaining power.

Will laws enacted by majority decisions of citizens be perfect? Far from it. But they will be much improved over the minority rule we now suffer. When people make mistakes, they will be more inclined to make corrections. That is not the case with representatives who are averse to admitting error for fear of having that information used against them in the next election.

I CONCLUDE THIS MANUSCRIPT with the simple observation that the answer to the problems of human governance lies with the people and not with their leaders. The design of representative government maintains citizens in civic adolescence. We want the largesse of government, but are reluctant to pay for it. We blame our elected officials when things go wrong, when, in fact, we are responsible for putting them in office. That is the definition of adolescence. By becoming lawmakers and becoming responsible for public policy, the consequences of which we will enjoy or suffer, we will facilitate our civic maturation—a human development that will benefit all facets of human life. Civic maturity is the most important result of turning to each other to exert control over our system of representative government.

The American dream envisioned in the Declaration of Independence is the vision of all human beings. We have yet to realize it in America, and when we do, I predict it will race around the world like the light of the sun. Cicero defined freedom as participation in power. The goal of this book and the purpose of my life are to help people understand how they can have freedom by promoting their participation in the power of government—lawmaking. It is our birthright, if we dare to claim it.

Appendix A

Democracy Amendment

Section 1. The sovereign authority and the legislative power of citizens of the United States to enact, repeal and amend public policy, laws, charters, and constitutions by local, state and national initiatives shall not be denied or abridged by the United States or any state.

Section 2. The citizens of the United States hereby sanction the national election conducted by the nonprofit corporation Philadelphia II, permitting the enactment of this Article and the Democracy Act.

Section 3. The United States Electoral Trust (hereinafter "Electoral Trust") is hereby created to administer the procedures established by this Article and the Democracy Act. A Board of Trustees and a Director shall govern the Electoral Trust. The Board of Trustees shall be composed of one member elected by the citizens of each state, the District of Columbia, Puerto Rico, and the Territories of the United States. An election shall be conducted every two years to elect members of the Board of Trustees. Immediately after the first election, the elected members shall be divided as equally as possible into two classes. The seats of the members of the first class shall be vacated at the expiration of the second year; the seats of the members of the second class shall be vacated at the expiration of the fourth year. All members of the Board of Trustees shall serve for four years except the members of the first class. In order to facilitate the initial election of members to the Board of Trustees, an Interim Board is appointed by the Democracy Act. A Director responsible for day-to-day operations shall be appointed by the majority of the members of the Board of Trustees, except that the first Director shall be appointed by the Board of Directors of Philadelphia II.

Section 4. An initiative created under the authority of this Article that modifies a constitution or charter assumes the force of law when it is approved by more than half the registered voters of the relevant jurisdiction in each of two successive elections conducted by the Electoral Trust. If such initiative is approved in the first election, the second election shall occur no earlier than six months and no later than a year after the first election. An initiative created under the authority of this Article that enacts, modifies or repeals any statute assumes the force of law when approved by more than half the registered voters of the relevant jurisdiction participating in an election conducted by the Electoral Trust.

Section 5. Only natural persons who are citizens of the United States may sponsor an initiative under the authority of this Article.

Section 6. Only natural persons who are citizens of the United States may contribute funds, services or property in support of or in opposition to a legislative initiative created under the authority of this Article. Contributions from corporations including, but not limited to, such incorporated entities as industry groups, labor unions, political parties, political action committees, organized religions and associations, are specifically prohibited. Such entities are also prohibited from coercing or inducing employees, clients, customers, members, or any other associated persons to support or oppose an initiative created under the authority of this Article.

Section 7. The people shall have the power to enforce the provisions of this Article by appropriate legislation. No court in the United States may enjoin an initiative election except on grounds of fraud.

Appendix B

The Democracy Act

AN ACT establishing legislative procedures and an administrative agency to permit the citizens of the United States to exercise their legislative power; and adding to the Federal Code.

Be It Enacted By the People of the United States:

Section 1. TITLE
This act shall be known and may be cited as the Democracy Act.

Section 2. PREAMBLE
We, the People of the United States, inherently possess the sovereign authority and power to govern ourselves. We asserted this power in our Declaration of Independence and in the ratification of our Constitution. We, the People, choose now to participate as lawmakers in our local, state and national governments. We, the People, sanction the election conducted by the nonprofit corporation Philadelphia II enabling our empowerment as lawmakers. We, the People, shall exercise our legislative powers by initiative concurrently with the legislative powers we delegated to our elected representatives. THEREFORE, We, the People, enact this Democracy Act, establishing a "Legislature of the People."

Section 3. PROCEDURES
The United States Electoral Trust (hereinafter "Electoral Trust") shall qualify initiatives chronologically and shall conduct the entire initiative process chronologically. The Electoral Trust shall take advantage of

contemporary technology in implementing these procedures. The essential elements of the initiative process include, but are not limited to, the following:

A. Sponsor

Only citizens of the United States who are registered to vote may sponsor an initiative. The Sponsor shall be identified on the initiative, on any petition, and on any qualifying poll.

B. Form

An initiative shall comprise a Title, a Summary, a Preamble that states the reasons for, and explains why, the initiative is proposed, and the complete text of the initiative.

C. Content

An initiative shall pertain to a matter of public policy relevant to the government jurisdiction to which it is applicable. The Sponsor shall determine the wording of the initiative. The Title and Summary shall be subject to the approval of the Electoral Trust.

D. Subject

An initiative shall address one subject only, but may include related or mutually dependent parts.

E. Word Limit

An initiative shall contain no more than five thousand words, exclusive of the Title, Preamble, Summary, References, Definitions, and language that quotes existing law.

F. Qualification

Following approval of the Title and Summary by the Electoral Trust, an initiative may qualify for election in the relevant government jurisdiction by any one of the following methods:

1) Citizen Petition

An initiative shall qualify for election if it is the subject of a petition signed manually or electronically by a number of registered voters, to be specified by the Electoral Trust, within the relevant government jurisdiction. The time period allotted to gather qualifying petition signatures shall be not more than two years, beginning on the date the first signature is collected.

2) Public Opinion Poll of Citizens

An initiative shall qualify for election if the subject matter described in the title and summary is approved in a public opinion poll. To qualify by this method, the polling plan, including the number of respondents, the methodology and the entity that will conduct the poll, shall be approved by the Electoral Trust.

3) Legislative Resolution

An initiative shall qualify for election if a resolution, the wording of which is identical to the initiative as submitted by its sponsor, is passed by simple majority in the legislative body of the relevant jurisdiction; except that, if the initiative proposes to create or alter a constitution or charter, such resolution must pass by a two-thirds majority.

G. Withdrawal

The Sponsor of an initiative may withdraw an initiative from further consideration and processing at any time prior to a deadline established by the Electoral Trust.

H. Public Hearing

After an initiative qualifies for election, the Electoral Trust shall appoint a Hearing Officer to conduct a public hearing on that initiative. Representatives of the Sponsor and representatives of the legislative body of the relevant jurisdiction shall participate in the hearing in accordance with policies and procedures established by the Electoral Trust. Testimony on the initiative by citizens, proponents, opponents, and experts shall be solicited and their testimony shall be published as the Hearing Record.

I. Deliberative Committee

After the public hearing on each initiative, the Electoral Trust shall convene a Deliberative Committee to review that initiative. The

Deliberative Committee shall consist of citizens selected at random from the voter registration rolls of the relevant jurisdiction maintained by the Electoral Trust. Members of the Deliberative Committee shall be fairly compensated for time spent and expenses incurred in performance of Committee duties. The Electoral Trust shall provide technical support and such additional resources as are necessary for the effective discharge of the Committee's duties. The Deliberative Committee shall review the Hearing Record, secure expert advice, deliberate the merits of the initiative, and prepare a written report of its deliberations and recommendations. By two-thirds vote, the Committee may alter the Title, Summary, Preamble or text of the initiative, provided that the changes are consistent with the stated purpose of the initiative.

J. Legislative Advisory Vote
Each initiative, together with its Hearing Record and report of the Deliberative Committee, shall be transmitted to the legislative body of the relevant jurisdiction. The legislative body shall conduct a public vote of its members, recording the yeas and nays on the initiative, within 90 days after receipt thereof. The vote of the legislative body is non-binding, serving only as an advisory to the citizens.

K. Election
Upon completion of the Legislative Advisory Vote, or 90 days after the initiative has been delivered to the legislative body of the relevant jurisdiction, whichever occurs first, the Electoral Trust shall publish a schedule for the election of the initiative and shall conduct an election in accordance with the published schedule.

L. Enactment
An initiative that creates or modifies a constitution or charter assumes the force of law when it is approved by more than half the registered voters in the relevant jurisdiction in each of two successive elections conducted by the Electoral Trust. If such initiative is approved in the first election, the second election shall occur no earlier than six months and no later than a year after, the first election. An initiative that enacts, modifies or repeals statute law assumes the force of law when approved by more than half the registered voters participating in an election conducted by the Electoral Trust in the relevant jurisdiction.

M. Effective Date

The effective date of an initiative, if not otherwise specified in the initiative, shall be forty-five days after certification of its enactment by the Electoral Trust.

N. Judicial Review

No court shall have the power to enjoin any initiative election except on grounds of fraud. After an initiative has been enacted into statute law, courts, when requested, may determine the constitutionality of the law. Courts have no power to adjudicate initiatives that amend the United States Constitution.

O. Promotional Communications

Any communication, regardless of the medium through which conveyed, that promotes or opposes an initiative shall conspicuously identify the person(s) responsible for that communication, in a manner specified by the Electoral Trust.

P. Campaign Financing

Only United States citizens may contribute funds, services or property in support of or in opposition to an initiative. Contributions from corporations including, but not limited to, such incorporated entities as industry groups, labor unions, political parties, political action committees, organized religions and associations, are specifically prohibited. Such entities are also prohibited from coercing or inducing employees, clients, customers, members, or any other associated persons to support or oppose an initiative. Violation of these prohibitions is a felony punishable by not more than one year in prison, or a fine not to exceed One Hundred Thousand Dollars, or both, per instance, applied to each person found guilty of the violation.

Q. Financial Disclosure

The Electoral Trust shall establish financial reporting requirements applicable to initiative sponsors, proponents and opponents, with monetary thresholds appropriate to the affected government jurisdiction. The Electoral Trust shall make all financial reports available to the public immediately upon its receipt thereof. Failure of sponsors, proponents or opponents to comply with these reporting requirements shall be a felony punishable by not more than one year in prison or a fine not to exceed One Hundred Thousand Dollars, or both, per instance, applied to each person found guilty of the violation.

Section 4. UNITED STATES ELECTORAL TRUST

The Electoral Trust shall administer the Democracy Amendment and the Democracy Act. The Electoral Trust shall be governed by a Board of Trustees and a Director. The Electoral Trust shall take advantage of contemporary technology in carrying out its mission. The activities of the Electoral Trust shall be transparent to the public.

A. Mission

The Electoral Trust shall impartially administer the Democracy Amendment and the Democracy Act, including the legislative procedures herein, so as to facilitate the exercise of the citizens' legislative power. The Electoral Trust shall ensure that citizens may file, qualify and vote on initiatives relevant to any government jurisdiction at any time and from any location. The Electoral Trust shall neither influence the outcome of any initiative, nor alter the substance of any initiative, except as specified in Section 3.I, "Deliberative Committee".

B. Board of Trustees

The Board of Trustees shall establish policy for and perform oversight of the Electoral Trust.

1) Membership

The Board of Trustees shall include 53 members: one member elected by the citizens of each of the 50 states, the District of Columbia, Puerto Rico and the Territories of the United States.

2) Term of Office

Members of the Board of Trustees shall serve a single four-year term except as follows: Immediately after the first election, the members shall be divided as equally as possible into two classes. The seats of the members of the first class shall be vacated at the expiration of the second year; the seats of the members of the second class shall be vacated at the expiration of the fourth year.

3) Removal of Trustees
Any member of the Board of Trustees shall be removed from office upon a three-fourths vote of the full membership of the Board of Trustees, or by a majority of the voters participating in a recall election in the political jurisdiction from which the member was elected.

4) Vacancies
A vacancy on the Board of Trustees shall be filled by majority vote of the full membership of the Board of Trustees on candidates who shall represent the political jurisdiction of the Trustee whose seat is vacant. A member appointed to fill a vacancy shall not subsequently be elected to the Board of Trustees.

5) Meetings
The Board of Trustees shall meet at least annually and at such other times and in such places as it deems appropriate to conduct its business. All meetings of the Board shall be publicized in advance and open to the public, except as required by law. The Electoral Trust shall publish the minutes and video recordings of all meetings of the Board, except as required by law.

C. Interim Board
The members of the Interim Board, hereby appointed, are the highest elected official (e.g., Lieutenant Governor, Secretary of State) responsible for the conduct of elections from each of the fifty states and Puerto Rico and the highest official responsible for the conduct of elections from the District of Columbia and the Territories of the United States. The responsibility and authority of this initial Board shall be confined to establishing policy and oversight for the registration of each citizen of the United States eligible to vote on an initiative, and establishing policy and oversight for the election of the members of the Board of Trustees.

D. Director

The Director of the Electoral Trust is the Chief Executive Officer of the Electoral Trust and is responsible for its day-to-day management and operations, consistent with the policies established by the Board of Trustees. The Director shall conduct the first election of the Board of Trustees as soon as possible.

1) Term of Office

The Director, except for the first Director, shall be appointed by majority vote of the Board of Trustees. The Director shall serve for a single term of six years. The Board of Directors of Philadelphia II shall appoint the first Director.

2) Removal of Director

The Director shall be removed from office upon a three-fourths vote of the full membership of the Board of Trustees, or by a majority of the voters participating in a national recall election.

3) Vacancy

A vacancy in the position of Director shall be filled by majority vote of the full membership of the Board of Trustees.

E. Oath or Affirmation of Office

Each Member of the Board of Trustees, the Interim Board, the Director and each employee of the Electoral Trust shall execute the following oath or affirmation of office as a condition of his or her service: "I, (name), (swear or affirm) that I will, to the best of my ability, defend and uphold the Constitution of the United States and the sovereign authority of the People to exercise their legislative power."

F. Organization and Responsibilities

The Electoral Trust shall staff and organize itself to fulfill its mission and shall develop policies, procedures and regulations to register citizens upon their becoming eligible to vote, to assist sponsors in preparing initiatives for qualification, to process initiatives, to administer initiative elections and to administer elections and recall elections of the Board of Trustees and recall elections of the Director. The Electoral Trust may select and contract for facilities and services, and prescribe staff duties and compensation. The Electoral Trust may also apply for and receive funds, and incur debt when necessary, and shall act in a responsible manner as a fiduciary agency of the People.

1) Existing Law

In fulfilling its responsibilities and performing its duties, the Electoral Trust shall comply with applicable laws and regulations of every government jurisdiction of the United States in which it operates that do not conflict with its mission defined in Section 4A, "Mission". Where laws are in conflict, this Democracy Act shall supersede.

2) Voter Registration

The Electoral Trust shall develop requirements, facilities and procedures for universal lifetime voter registration of citizens of the United States which shall be binding in elections conducted under the authority of the Democracy Amendment and this Act in every government jurisdiction in which a voter is, or may become, a legal resident.

3) Research and Drafting Service

The Electoral Trust shall establish and operate a legislative research and drafting service to assist citizens in preparing initiatives.

4) Communication

The Electoral Trust shall establish the means, procedures and regulations to facilitate the communication of timely, comprehensive, balanced, and pertinent information on the subject matter of each initiative, which information shall be conveyed to the citizens of the relevant jurisdiction by various media, including radio, television, print, and the Internet and/or other electronic media. The Electoral Trust shall establish and maintain a web site for each qualified initiative that will contain, at a minimum, a summary of the Hearing Record, the report of the Deliberative Committee, the result of the Legislative Advisory Vote, statements prepared by the Sponsor, other proponents and opponents, and a balanced analysis prepared by the Electoral Trust of the pros and cons of the initiative, its societal, environmental, and economic implications, costs and benefits.

5) Hearings and Deliberative Committees

The Electoral Trust shall organize a Hearing to receive testimony and shall convene a Deliberative Committee to deliberate on each qualified initiative. The Electoral Trust shall provide or arrange for professional Hearing Officers and Deliberation Facilitators, technical consultants and support staff and facilities as needed for the effective conduct of Hearings and Committee activities.

6) Elections

The Electoral Trust shall devise and administer policies and procedures to conduct elections of initiatives, of the Board of Trustees, and for the recall of any Trustee or the Director. In doing so, it shall take advantage of contemporary technology in developing procedures for voting and validating votes. All such policies and procedures shall be neutral with respect to the content of initiatives administered and the outcomes of elections conducted.

G. Budgets

Budgets covering all elements of the Electoral Trust's operations and activities shall be prepared and published consistent with government practices and the public nature of the Electoral Trust's responsibilities.

Section 5. APPROPRIATIONS

The People hereby authorize the appropriation of funds from the Treasury of the United States, pursuant to Article I, Section 9(7) of the United States Constitution, to enable the Electoral Trust to organize itself, repay debts herein described, and begin the performance of its duties. Debts to be repaid under this Section are those incurred by Philadelphia II, the proceeds of which were used to pay the costs of preparing for and conducting the election for the enactment of the National Initiative for Democracy, which costs shall include, but shall not be limited to, the production cost of ballots, printing, mail, print and electronic communications, including the Internet, and services in support of the election conducted by Philadelphia II, and related costs such as the cost of the legal defense of Philadelphia II's operations, all of which shall have been audited and certified as bona fide by the

Electoral Trust prior to repayment. Hereafter, appropriations shall be made annually to the Electoral Trust as an independent agency of the United States Government.

Section 6. SEVERABILITY
In the event that any one or more of the provisions of this Act shall for any reason be held to be invalid as a result of judicial action, the remaining provisions of this Act shall be unimpaired.

Section 7. ENACTMENT BY THE PEOPLE

A. The Ballot
Philadelphia II shall present a ballot to the citizens of the United States for their legislative decision on the enactment of the National Initiative for Democracy by direct contact, mail, print, Internet and/or other media. Regardless of the media through which they are presented and transmitted, all ballots shall provide for entry of the following information:

- The voter's name.
- The voter's address, including street, city, postal code, county and state of residence.
- The voter's telephone number.
- The voter's e-mail address.
- A Yes or No vote on the National Initiative for Democracy.
- The date the ballot is executed.
- The voter's Identification Number (provided by Philadelphia II).
- The voter's Password (provided by Philadelphia II).
- The physical or electronic signature of the voter.

B. The Election
Citizens registered to vote in any government jurisdiction within the United States may participate in the election for the National Initiative by executing a ballot such as described above and conveying it to Philadelphia II. The Amendment shall have been ratified and the Democracy Act enacted when Philadelphia II has received a number

of affirmative votes greater than half the total number of government-validated votes cast in the presidential election occurring immediately prior to this election's certification by the President of Philadelphia II to the government of the United States, provided that the number of affirmative votes exceeds the number of negative votes received by Philadelphia II at that time.

Section 8. DEFINITIONS

Administer
Plan, manage and execute the operations of an organization in accordance with governing policy, organizational regulations and pertinent constitutional and statute law.

Appropriation
A legislative act of the U.S. House of Representatives transferring public funds from the United States Treasury, in accordance with Article I, Section 9(7) of the Constitution.

Authorize (an appropriation)
A legislative act to empower or give necessary authority to make an appropriation of public funds from the United States Treasury.

Ballot
A document listing alternatives to be voted on or questions to be answered, along with other pertinent information. In this context, the ballot requests a simple "Yes" or "No" vote on the National Initiative for Democracy, plus information allowing verification of the voter's registration status together with data that can be used to contact the voter to confirm that his or her vote was accurately recorded.

Budget
An itemized summary of anticipated income and intended expenditures for a specified period of time.

Campaign

An operation or related set of operations pursued to accomplish a political purpose. In this context it refers to all of the activities conducted by any citizen or group of citizens together with all the resources applied by them to the goal of enacting or defeating an initiative.

Certify/Certification

To confirm formally as to truth, accuracy, or genuineness; to guarantee as having met a standard. In this context:

- Citizens who vote to enact the National Initiative will certify their status as registered voters; and
- the Electoral Trust will certify the results of an election as being true and accurate, and having conformed to the law governing initiative elections; and
- Philadelphia II will certify to the United States government that, as a result of a national election, the Democracy Amendment and the Democracy Act are the law of the land.

Charter

A document that has been ratified by the people effected to establish and define the fundamental powers and privileges of a governing body for a municipality, county or other corporation.

Chief Executive Officer

The executive with responsibility and authority to plan, manage and conduct the operations of an organization; including the appointment of subordinate managers, hiring of employees, contracting for services, and undertaking or overseeing all other activities necessary to fulfill the mission of the organization subject to policies and guidelines established by the governing board of the organization or other superior authority.

Citizen

A person entitled by birth or naturalization to the protection of a state or nation; in particular, one entitled to vote and enjoy other privileges.

Coerce
To force to act in a certain way by use of pressure, threats, or intimidation.

Deliberation Facilitator
A professional in group processes and the effective conduct of meetings who is made available by the Electoral Trust to assist the citizen members of a Deliberative Committee in the conduct of their deliberations.

Election
In this context, the entire process, and the infrastructure supporting that process, by which votes are cast and tabulated to determine whether or not an initiative has been approved or rejected by the voters; or the process by which votes are cast and tabulated to determine the membership of the Board of Trustees of the Electoral Trust.

File (an initiative)
An initiative is filed when the Sponsor submits the initiative to the Electoral Trust for approval of its Title and Summary.

Government
Government (local, state or national) A governing body that is defined by and draws its authority from a constitution or charter.

Government Jurisdiction
A geographic area subject to governance by a legislative body. In this context, national, state, county or equivalent (e.g., parish), municipality (e.g., cities and towns), commonwealth (i.e., Puerto Rico) and Trust Territory (i.e., American Samoa, Guam and Virgin Islands), plus the District of Columbia—are the specific jurisdictions referred to and included under the Democracy Act.

Induce
In this context, to lead or move, as to a course of action, by promise of reward or consideration.

Initiative
The legislative instrument chosen by the voting citizens of the United States to exercise their inherent power to enact or modify any governmental policy, law, charter, or constitution; as set forth in the Democracy Amendment to the U.S. Constitution.

Initiative Process
Infrastructure and procedures by which legislation may be introduced and enacted directly by the people.

Jurisdiction
See "Government Jurisdiction."

Lawmaker/Legislator
One who makes or enacts laws. In this context, either a member of an elected legislative body such as Congress, a state legislature, or a city council; or a citizen eligible to vote in the Legislature of the People.

Legislation
A legislative resolution or statute law produced by a legislature.

Legislative Advisory Vote
A legally non-binding vote required by the Democracy Act to be taken by the legislative body of the government jurisdiction affected by an initiative, in which the members of the elected legislature publicly vote yea or nay on the initiative. Serves as an advisory or cue to the citizens.

Legislative Body
An elected group of individuals having the power to create, amend and repeal laws together with the policies, procedures and infrastructure established by and under a governing constitution or charter.

Legislative Resolution
A formal expression of the opinion or "will" of a legislative body.

Legislature

An officially elected or otherwise selected body of people vested with the responsibility and power to make laws for a political unit, such as a state or nation.

Legislature of the People

The body of citizens who are eligible to vote in an election conducted by the Electoral Trust, which administers the policies, procedures and infrastructure established by and under the authority of the Democracy Amendment and the Democracy Act.

National Initiative

Short title for the National Initiative for Democracy.

National Initiative for Democracy

The Democracy Amendment to the Constitution of the United States and the Democracy Act, packaged together for concurrent presentation to the citizens of the United States in a national election to be conducted by Philadelphia II.

Opponent (of an initiative)

Any person who attempts, by any action, including but not limited to the contribution of funds, services, or other resources to be used for the creation or dissemination of information, to advocate that a qualified initiative be defeated at election.

Petition

In this context, a document in which registered voters indicate that they wish an initiative to be qualified for election. Petitions may be hard copy or electronic documents, and may be signed manually or electronically.

Philadelphia II

The non-profit corporation conducting the election for the National Initiative.

Poll

In this context, a validated sampling of registered voters in which the respondents indicate whether or not they wish an initiative to be qualified for election.

Polling Plan

A document that describes the number and source of respondents; the method by which the respondents for a poll will be drawn; how the data will be collected, tabulated and presented; and how the question(s) on the poll will be worded. The Electoral Trust may require a polling plan to include such additional information as will permit it to carry out its responsibility to determine if the planned poll will accurately reflect the views of the citizens in the government jurisdiction affected by the initiative addressed by the proposed poll.

Proponent (of an initiative)

Any person who attempts, by any action, including but not limited to the contribution of funds, services, or other resources to be used for the creation or dissemination of information, to advocate that a qualified initiative be enacted at election.

Qualify (an initiative)

To qualify for election an initiative must meet criteria established by the Democracy Act, thereby enabling the Electoral Trust to begin the processing of the initiative that leads to its enactment or defeat in an election by registered voters.

Ratify

An act of approval by a sovereign authority.

Registered Voter

In this context, any citizen of the United States who is at least 18 years old, who has registered once in his or her lifetime, is not imprisoned for a felony, and who has not been classified as "incompetent" by a court, provided that he or she has not renounced or otherwise given up United States citizenship.

Signature, Electronic

"Electronic signature" is a generic, technology-neutral term that refers to the result of any of the various methods by which one can "sign" an electronic document. Examples of electronic signatures include: a digitized image of a handwritten signature, a secret code or personal identification number (PIN) (such as are used with ATM cards and credit cards) or a unique biometrics-based identifier, such as a fingerprint or a retinal scan. The Electoral Trust will specify and/or implement electronic signature technology to be used by voters who choose to submit ballots signed electronically.

Signature, Manual

A person's name or equivalent mark written in the person's own handwriting.

Sovereign

When used as a noun: one who, singly or in company with others, possesses supreme authority in a nation or other governmental unit. When used as an adjective: self-governing; independent; possessing highest authority and jurisdiction.

Sponsor

A person or a group of individually identified people, responsible for the submission of an initiative to the Electoral Trust for qualification and processing.

Statute Law

An enactment by a legislative body, e.g., laws, resolutions and ordinances.

The People of the United States

The introductory phrase of the Democracy Act begins with the phrase "Be It Enacted By The People Of The United States." In this context the term "People of the United States" is used for consistency with our Constitution and Declaration of Independence.

Transparency, Transparent
In general usage: free from guile; candid, open and easily understood. In this context, the term "transparent" refers to the fact that the workings and products of the Electoral Trust are to be continuously public; that is, open to inspection and review by the citizenry except as may be required by law.

Appendix C

The Declaration of Independence

IN CONGRESS, JULY 4, 1776
The unanimous Declaration of the thirteen united States of America

When in the course of human events it becomes necessary for one people to dissolve the political bands which have connected them with another and to assume among the powers of the earth, the separate and equal station to which the laws of nature and of nature's God entitle them, a decent respect to the opinions of mankind requires that they should declare the causes which impel them to the separation.

We hold these truths to be self-evident, that all men are created equal, that they are endowed by their Creator with certain unalienable rights; that among these are life, liberty and the pursuit of happiness.

–That to secure these rights, governments are instituted among men, deriving their just powers from the consent of the governed.

–That whenever any form of government becomes destructive of these ends, it is the right of the people to alter or to abolish it, and to institute new government, laying its foundations on such principles and organizing its powers in such form, as to them shall seem most likely to effect their safety and happiness. Prudence, indeed, will dictate that governments long established should not be changed for light and transient causes; and accordingly all experience hath shown that mankind are more disposed to suffer, while evils are sufferable than to right themselves by abolishing the forms to which they are accustomed. But when a long train of abuses and usurpations, pursuing invariably the same object evinces a design to reduce them under absolute despotism, it is their right, it is their duty, to throw off such government, and to provide new guards for their future security.

—Such has been the patient sufferance of these colonies; and such is now the necessity which constrains them to alter their former systems of government. The history of the present King of Great Britain is a history of repeated injuries and usurpations, all having in direct object the establishment of an absolute tyranny over these states. To prove this, let facts be submitted to a candid world.

He has refused his assent to laws, the most wholesome and necessary for the public good.

He has forbidden his governors to pass laws of immediate and pressing importance, unless suspended in their operation till his assent should be obtained; and when so suspended, he has utterly neglected to attend to them.

He has refused to pass other laws for the accommodation of large districts of people, unless those people would relinquish the right of representation in the legislature, a right inestimable to them and formidable to tyrants only.

He has called together legislative bodies at places unusual, uncomfortable, and distant from the depository of their public records, for the sole purpose of fatiguing them into compliance with his measures.

He has dissolved representative houses repeatedly, for opposing with manly firmness his invasions on the rights of the people.

He has refused for along time, after such dissolutions, to cause others to be elected, whereby the legislative powers, incapable of annihilation, have returned to the people at large for their exercise; the state remaining in the mean time exposed to all the dangers of invasion from without, and convulsions within.

He has endeavored to prevent the population of these states; for that purpose obstructing the laws of naturalization of foreigners; refusing to pass others to encourage their migrations hither, and raising the conditions of new appropriations of lands.

He has obstructed the administration of justice by refusing his assent to laws for establishing judiciary powers.

He has made judges dependent on his will alone for the tenure of their offices, and the amount and payment of their salaries.

He has erected a multitude of new offices, and sent hither swarms of officers to harass our people and eat out their substance.

He has kept among us, in times of peace, standing armies without the consent of our legislatures.

He has affected to render the military independent of and superior to the civil power.

He has combined with others to subject us to a jurisdiction foreign to our constitution, and unacknowledged by our laws; giving his assent to their acts of pretended legislation:

For quartering large bodies of armed troops among us;

For protecting them, by a mock trial from punishment for any murders which they should commit on the inhabitants of these states;

For cutting off our trade with all parts of the world;

For imposing taxes on us without our consent;

For depriving us, in many cases, of the benefit of trial by jury;

For transporting us beyond seas to be tried for pretended offenses;

For abolishing the free system of English laws in a neighboring province, establishing therein an arbitrary government, and enlarging its boundaries so as to render it at once an example and fit instrument for introducing the same absolute rule into these colonies;

For taking away our charters, abolishing our most valuable laws and altering fundamentally the forms of our governments;

For suspending our own legislatures and declaring themselves invested with power to legislate for us in all cases whatsoever.

He has abdicated government here, by declaring us out of his protection and waging war against us.

He has plundered our seas, ravaged our coasts, burnt our towns, and destroyed the lives of our people.

He is at this time transporting large armies of foreign mercenaries to complete the works of death, desolation, and tyranny, already begun with circumstances of cruelty and perfidy scarcely paralleled in the most barbarous ages, and totally unworthy the head of a civilized nation.

He has constrained our fellow citizens taken captive on the high seas to bear arms against their country, to become the executioners of their friends and brethren, or to fall themselves by their hands.

He has excited domestic insurrections amongst us, and has endeavored to bring on the inhabitants of our frontiers, the merciless

Indian savages whose known rule of warfare is an undistinguished destruction of all ages, sexes and conditions.

In every stage of these oppressions we have petitioned for redress in the most humble terms: Our repeated petitions have been answered only by repeated injury. A prince, whose character is thus marked by every act which may define a tyrant, is unfit to be the ruler of a free people.

Nor have we been wanting in attentions to our British brethren. We have warned them from time to time of attempts by their legislature to extend an unwarrantable jurisdiction over us. We have reminded them of the circumstances of our emigration and settlement here. We have appealed to their native justice and magnanimity, and we have conjured them by the ties of our common kindred to disavow these usurpations, which would inevitably interrupt our connections and correspondence. They too have been deaf to the voice of justice and of consanguinity. We must, therefore, acquiesce in the necessity, which denounces our separation, and hold them, as we hold the rest of mankind, enemies in war, in peace friends.

We, therefore, the representatives of the united states of America, in general congress, assembled, appealing to the supreme judge of the world for the rectitude of our intentions, do, in the name, and by authority of the good people of these colonies, solemnly publish and declare that these united colonies are, and of right ought to be, free and independent states, that they are absolved from all allegiance to the British Crown, and that all political connection between them and the State of Great Britain, is and ought to be totally dissolved; and that as free and independent states, they have full power to levy war, conclude peace, contract alliances, establish commerce, and to do all other acts and things, which independent states may of right do. –And for this Declaration, with a firm reliance on the protection of Divine Providence, we mutually pledge to each other our lives, our fortunes, and our sacred honor.

Appendix D

The United States Constitution

Preamble

We the People of the United States, in Order to form a more perfect Union, establish Justice, insure domestic tranquility, provide for the common defence, promote the general Welfare, and secure the Blessings of Liberty to ourselves and our Posterity, do ordain and establish this Constitution for the United States of America.

Article. I.

Section. 1.
All legislative Powers herein granted shall be vested in a Congress of the United States, which shall consist of a Senate and a House of Representatives.

Section. 2.
The House of Representatives shall be composed of Members chosen every second Year by the People of the several States, and the Electors in each State shall have the Qualifications requisite for Electors of the most numerous Branch of the State Legislature.

No Person shall be a Representative who shall not have attained to the Age of twenty five Years, and been seven Years a Citizen of the United States, and who shall not, when elected, be an inhabitant of that State in which he shall be chosen.

Representatives and direct Taxes shall be apportioned among the several States which may be included within this Union, according to their respective Numbers, which shall be determined by adding to the whole Number of free Persons, including those bound to Service for a Term of Years, and excluding Indians not taxed, three fifths of all other Persons. The actual Enumeration shall be made within three Years after the first Meeting of the Congress of the United States, and within every subsequent Term of ten years, in such Manner as they shall by Law direct. The Number of Representatives shall not exceed one for every thirty Thousand, but each State shall have at Least one Representative; and until such enumeration shall be made, the State of New Hampshire shall be entitled to chuse three, Massachusetts eight, Rhode-Island and Providence Plantations one, Connecticut five, New-York six, New Jersey four, Pennsylvania eight, Delaware one, Maryland six, Virginia ten, North Carolina five, South Caroline five, and Georgia three.

When vacancies happen in the Representation from any State, the Executive Authority thereof shall issue Writs of Election to fill such Vacancies.

The House of Representatives shall chuse their Speaker and other Officers; and shall have the sole Power of Impeachment.

Section. 3.
The Senate of the United States shall be composed of two Senators from each State, chosen by the Legislature thereof for six Years; and each Senator shall have one Vote.

Immediately after they shall be assembled in Consequence of the first Election, they shall be divided as equally as may be into three Classes. The Seats of the Senators of the first Class shall be vacated at the Expiration of the second Year, of the second Class at the Expiration of the fourth Year, and of the third Class at the Expiration of the sixth Year, so that one third may be chosen every second year; and if Vacancies happen by Resignation, or otherwise, during the Recess of the Legislature of any State, the Executive thereof may make temporary Appointments until the next meeting of the Legislature, which shall then fill such Vacancies.

No Person shall be a Senator who shall not have attained to the Age of thirty Years, and been nine Years a Citizen of the United States, and who shall not, when elected, be an Inhabitant of that State for which he shall be chosen.

The Vice President of the United States shall be President of the Senate, but shall have no Vote, unless they be equally divided.

The Senate shall chuse their other Officers, and also a President pro tempore, in the Absence of the Vice President, or when he shall exercise the office of President of the United States.

The Senate shall have the sole Power to try all Impeachments. When sitting for that Purpose, they shall be on Oath or Affirmation. When the President of the United States is tried, the Chief justice shall preside: And no Person shall be convicted without the Concurrence of two thirds of the Members present.

Judgment in Cases of Impeachment shall not extend further than to removal from Office, and disqualification to hold and enjoy any Office of honor, Trust or Profit under the United States: but the Party convicted shall nevertheless be liable and subject to Indictment, Trial, Judgment and Punishment, according to Law.

Section. 4.

The Times, Places and Manner of holding Elections for Senators and Representatives, shall be prescribed in each State by the Legislature thereof; but the Congress may at any time by Law make or alter such Regulations, except as to the Places of chusing Senators.

The Congress shall assemble at least once in every Year, and such Meeting shall be on the first Monday in December, unless they shall by Law appoint a different Day.

Section. 5.

Each House shall be the Judge of the Elections, Returns and Qualifications of its own Members, and a Majority of each shall constitute a Quorum to do Business; but a smaller Number may adjourn from day to day, and may be authorized to compel the Attendance of absent Members, in such Manner, and under such Penalties as each House may provide.

Each House may determine the Rules of its Proceedings, punish its Members for disorderly Behaviour, and, with the concurrence of two thirds, expel a Member.

Each House shall keep a Journal of its Proceedings, and from time to time publish the same, excepting such Parts as may in their Judgment require Secrecy; and the Yeas and Nays of the Members of either House on any question shall, at the Desire of one firth of those Present, be entered into the Journal.

Neither House, during the Session of Congress, shall, without the Consent of the other, adjourn for more than three days, nor to any other Place than that in which the two Houses shall be sitting.

Section. 6.
The Senators and Representatives shall receive a Compensation for their Services, to be ascertained by Law, and paid out of the Treasury of the United States. They shall in all Cases, except Treason, Felony and Breach of the Peace, be privileged from Arrest during their Attendance at the Session of their respective Houses, and in going to and returning from the same; and for any Speech or Debate in either House, they shall not be questioned in any other Place.

No Senator or Representative shall, during the Time for which he was elected, be appointed to any civil Office under the Authority of the United States, which shall have been created, or the Emoluments whereof shall have been encreased during such time; and no Person holding any Office under the United States, shall be a Member of either House during his Continuance in Office.

Section. 7.
All Bills for raising Revenue shall originate in the House of Representatives; but the Senate may propose or concur with Amendments as on other Bills.

Every Bill which shall have passed the House of Representatives and the Senate, shall, before it become a Law, be presented to the President of the United States: If he approve he shall sign it, but if not he shall return it, with his Objections to that House in which it shall have originated, who shall enter the Objections at large on their Journal, and proceed to reconsider it. If after such Reconsideration two thirds of that House shall agree to pass the Bill, it shall be sent, together with the Objections, to the other House, by which it shall likewise be reconsidered, and if approved by two thirds of that House, it shall become a Law. But in all such Cases the Votes of both Houses shall be determined by yeas and Nays, and the Names of the Persons voting for and against the Bill shall be entered on the Journal of each House respectively. If any Bill shall not be returned by the President within ten Days (Sundays excepted) after it shall have been presented to him, the Same shall be a Law, in like Manner as if he had signed it, unless the Congress by their Adjournment prevent its Return, in which Case it shall not be a Law.

Every Order, Resolution, or Vote to which the Concurrence of the Senate and House of Representatives may be necessary (except on a question of Adjournment) shall be presented to the President of the United States; and before the Same shall take Effect, shall be approved by him, or being disapproved by him, shall be repassed by two thirds of the Senate and House of Representatives, according to the Rules and Limitations prescribed in the Case of a Bill.

Section. 8.

The Congress shall have Power To lay and collect Taxes, Duties, Imposts and Excises, to pay the Debts and provide for the common Defence and general Welfare of the United States; but all Duties, Imposts and Excises shall be uniform throughout the United States;

To borrow Money on the credit of the United States;

To regulate Commerce with foreign Nations, and among the several States, and with the Indian Tribes;

To establish an uniform Rule of Naturalization, and uniform Laws on the subject of Bankruptcies throughout the United States;

To coin Money, regulate the Value thereof, and of foreign Coin, and fix the Standard of Weights and Measures;

To provide for the Punishment of counterfeiting the Securities and current Coin of the United States;

To establish Post Offices and post Roads;

To promote the Progress of Science and useful Arts, by securing for limited Times to Authors and Inventors the exclusive Right to their respective Writings and Discoveries;

To constitute Tribunals inferior to the Supreme Court;

To define and punish Piracies and Felonies committed on the high Seas, and Offences against the Law of Nations;

To declare War, grant Letters of Marque and Reprisal, and make Rules concerning Captures on Land and Water;

To raise and support Armies, but no Appropriation of Money to that Use shall be for a longer Term than two Years;

To provide and maintain a Navy;

To make Rules for the Government and Regulation of the land and naval Forces;

To provide for calling forth the Militia to execute the Laws of the Union, suppress insurrections and repel invasions;

To provide for organizing, arming, and disciplining, the Militia, and for governing such Part of them as may be employed in the Service of the United States, reserving to the States respectively, the Appointment of the Officers, and the Authority of training the Militia according to the discipline prescribed by Congress.

To exercise exclusive Legislation in all Cases whatsoever, over such District (not exceeding ten Miles square) as may, by Cession of particular States, and the Acceptance of Congress, become the Seat of the Government of the United States, and to exercise like Authority over all Places purchases by the Consent of the Legislature of the State in which the Same shall be, for the Erection of Forts, Magazines, Arsenals, dock-Yards, and other needful Buildings;—And

To make all Laws which shall be necessary and proper for carrying into Execution the foregoing Powers, and all other Powers vested by this Constitution in the Government of the United States, or in any Department or Officer thereof.

Section. 9.
The Migration or Importation of such Persons as any of the States now existing shall think proper to admit, shall not be prohibited by the Congress prior to the Year one thousand eight hundred and eight, but a Tax or duty may be imposed on such importation, not exceeding ten dollars for each Person.

The Privilege of the Writ of Habeas Corpus shall not be suspended, unless when in Cases of Rebellion or Invasion of the public Safety may require it.

No Bill of Attainder or ex post facto Law shall be passed.

No Capitation, or other direct, Tax shall be laid, unless in Proportion to the Census or enumeration herein before directed to be taken.

No Tax or Duty shall be laid on Articles exported from any State.

No Preference shall be given by any Regulation of Commerce or Revenue to the Ports of one State over those of another; nor shall Vessels bound to, or from, one State, be obliged to enter, clear, or pay Duties in another.

No Money shall be drawn from the Treasury, but in Consequence of Appropriations made by Law; and a regular Statement and Account of the Receipts and Expenditures of all public Money shall be published from time to time.

No Title of Nobility shall be granted by the United States: And no Person holding any Office of Profit or Trust under them, shall, without the Consent of the Congress, accept of any present, Emolument, Office, or Title, of any kind whatever, from any King, Prince, or foreign State.

Section. 10.
No State shall enter into any Treaty, Alliance, or Confederation; grant Letters of Marque and Reprisal; coin Money; emit Bills of Credit; make any Thing but gold and silver Coin a Tender in Payment of Debts; pass any Bill of Attainder, ex post facto Law, or Law Impairing the Obligation of Contracts, or grant any Title of Nobility.

No State shall, without the Consent of the Congress, lay any imposts or Duties on Imports or Exports, except what may be absolutely necessary for executing it's inspection Laws: and the net Produce of all Duties and Imposts, laid by any State on Imports or Exports, shall be for the Use of the Treasury of the United States; and all such Laws shall be subject to the Revision and Controul of the Congress.

No State shall, without the Consent of Congress, lay any Duty of Tonnage, keep Troops, or Ships of War in time of Peace, enter into any Agreement or Compact with another State, or with a foreign Power, or engage in War, unless actually invaded, or in such imminent Danger as will not admit of delay.

Article. II.

Section 1.
The executive Power shall be vested in a President of the United States of America. He shall hold his Office during the Term, be elected, as follows:

Each State shall appoint, in such Manner as the Legislature thereof may direct, a Number of Electors, equal to the whole Number of Senators and Representatives to which the State may be entitled in the Congress: but no Senator or Representative, or Person holding an Office of Trust or Profit under the United States, shall be appointed an Elector.

The Electors shall meet in their respective States, and vote by Ballot for two persons, of whom one at least shall not be an inhabitant of the same State with themselves. And they shall make a List of all the Persons voted for, and of the Number of Votes for each; which List they shall sign and certify, and transmit sealed to the Seat of the Government of the United States, directed to the President of the Senate. The President of the Senate shall, in the Presence of the Senate and House of Representatives, open all the Certificates, and the Votes shall then be counted. The Person having the greatest Number of Votes shall be the President, if such Number be a Majority of the whole Number of Electors appointed; and if there be more than one who have such Majority, and have an equal Number of Votes, then the House of Representatives shall immediately chuse by Ballot one of them for President; and if no Person have a Majority, then from the five highest on the List the said House shall in like Manner chuse the President. But in chusing the President, the Votes shall be taken by States, the Representation from each State having one Vote; A quorum for this purpose shall consist of a Member or Members from two thirds of the States, and a Majority of all the States shall be necessary to a Choice. In every Case, after the Choice of the President, the Person having the greatest Number of Votes of the Electors shall be the Vice President. But if there should remain two or more who have equal Votes, the Senate shall chuse from them by Ballot the Vice President.

The Congress may determine the Time of chusing the Electors, and the Day on which they shall give their Votes; which Day shall be the same throughout the United States.

No person except a natural born Citizen, or a Citizen of the United States, at the time of the Adoption of this Constitution, shall be eligible to the Office of President; neither shall any Person be eligible to that

Office who shall not have attained the Age of thirty five Years, and been fourteen Years a resident within the United States.

In Case of the Removal of the President from office, or of his Death, Resignation, or inability to discharge the Powers and Duties of the said office, the Same shall devolve on the Vice President, and the Congress may by Law provide for the Case of Removal, Death, Resignation or Inability, both of the President and Vice President, declaring what Officer shall then act as President, and such Officer shall act accordingly, until the Disability be removed, or a President shall be elected.

The President shall, at stated Times, receive for his Services, a Compensation, which shall neither be increased nor diminished during the Period for which he shall have been elected, and he shall not receive within that Period any other Emolument from the United States, or any of them.

Before he enter on the Execution of his Office, he shall take the following Oath or Affirmation:—"I do solemnly swear (or affirm) that I will faithfully execute the Office of President of the United States, and will to the best of my Ability, preserve, protect and defend the Constitution of the United States."

Section. 2.
The President shall be Commander in Chief of the Army and Navy of the United States, and of the Militia of the several States, when called into the actual Service of the United States; he may require the Opinion, in writing, of the principal Officer in each of the executive Departments, upon any Subject relating to the Duties of their respective Offices, and he shall have Power to grant Reprieves and Pardons for Offences against the United States, except in Cases of Impeachment.

He shall have Power, by and with the Advice and Consent of the Senate, to make Treaties, provided two thirds of the Senators present concur; and he shall nominate, and by and with the Advice and Consent of the Senate, shall appoint Ambassadors, other public Ministers and Consuls, Judges of the supreme Court, and all other Officers of the

United States, whose Appointments are not herein otherwise provided for, and which shall be established by Law: but the Congress may by Law vest the Appointment of such inferior Officers, as they think proper, in the President alone, in the Courts of Law, or in the Heads of Departments.

The President shall have Power to fill up all Vacancies that may happen during the Recess of the Senate, by granting Commissions which shall expire at the End of their next Session.

Section. 3.

He shall from time to time give the Congress Information of the State of the Union, and recommend to their Consideration such measures as he shall judge necessary and expedient; he may, on extraordinary Occasions, convene both Houses, or either of them, and in Case of Disagreement between them, with Respect to the Time of Adjournment, he may adjourn them to such Time as he shall think proper; he shall receive Ambassadors and other public Ministers; he shall take Care that the Laws be faithfully executed, and shall Commission all the Officers of the United States.

Section. 4.

The President, Vice President and all civil Officers of the United States, shall be removed from Office on Impeachment for, and Conviction of, Treason, Bribery, or other high Crimes and Misdemeanors.

Article III.

Section. 1.

The judicial Power of the United States shall be vested in one supreme Court, and in such inferior Courts as the Congress may from time to time ordain and establish. The Judges, both of the supreme and inferior Courts, shall hold their Offices during good Behaviour, and shall, at stated Times, receive for their Services a Compensation, which shall not be diminished during their Continuance in office.

Section. 2.

The judicial Power shall extend to all Cases, in Law and Equity, arising under this Constitution, the Laws of the United States, and Treaties made, or which shall be made, under their Authority;—to all Cases affecting Ambassadors, other public Ministers and Consuls;—to all Cases of admiralty and maritime Jurisdiction;—to Controversies to which the United States shall be a Party;—to Controversies between two or more States;—between a State and Citizens of another States;—between Citizens of different States;—between Citizens of the same State claiming Lands under Grants of different States, and between a State, or the Citizens thereof, and foreign States, Citizens or Subjects.

In all Cases affecting Ambassadors, other public Ministers and Consuls, and those in which a State shall be Party, the supreme Court shall have original Jurisdiction. In all the other Cases before mentioned, the supreme Court shall have appellate Jurisdiction, both as to Law and Fact, with such Exceptions, and under such Regulations as the Congress shall make.

The Trial of all Crimes, except in Cases of Impeachment, shall be by Jury; and such Trial shall be held in the State where the said Crimes shall have been committed; but when not committed within any State, the Trial shall be at such Place or Places as the Congress may by Law have directed.

Section. 3.

Treason against the United States, shall consist only in levying War against them, or in adhering to their Enemies, giving them Aid and Comfort. No Person shall be convicted of Treason unless on the Testimony of two Witnesses to the same overt Act, or in Confession in open Court.

The Congress shall have Power to declare the Punishment of Treason, but no Attainder of Treasons shall work Corruption of Blood, or Forfeiture except during the Life of the Person attainted.

Article. IV.

Section. 1.
Full Faith and Credit shall be given in each State to the public Acts, Records, and judicial Proceedings of every other State. And the Congress may by general Laws prescribe the Manner in which such Acts, Records and Proceedings shall be proved, and the Effect thereof.

Section. 2.
The Citizens of each State shall be entitled to all Privileges and Immunities of Citizens in the several States.

A Person charged in any State with Treason, Felony, or other Crime, who shall flee from justice, and be found in another State, shall on Demand of the executive Authority of the State from which he fled, be delivered up, to be removed to the State having Jurisdiction of the Crime.

No Person held to Service or Labour in one State, under the Laws thereof, escaping into another, shall, in Consequence of any Law or Regulation therein, be discharged from such Service or Labour, but shall be delivered up on Claim of the Party to whom such Service or Labour may be due.

Section. 3.
New States may be admitted by the Congress to this Union; but no new State shall be formed or erected within the Jurisdiction of any other State; nor any State be formed by the Junction of two or more States, or Parts of States, without the Consent of the Legislatures of the States concerned as well as of the Congress.

The Congress shall have Power to dispose of and make all needful Rules and Regulations respecting the Territory or other Property belonging to the United States; and nothing in this Constitution shall be so construed as to Prejudice any Claims of the United States, or of any particular State.

Section. 4.

The United States shall guarantee to every State in this Union a Republican Form of Government, and shall protect each of them against invasion; and on Application of the Legislature, or of the Executive (when the Legislature cannot be convened), against domestic Violence.

Article. V.

The Congress, whenever two thirds of both Houses shall deem it necessary, shall propose Amendments to this Constitution, or, on the Application of the Legislatures of two thirds of the several States, shall call a Convention for proposing Amendments, which, in either Case, shall be valid to all Intents and Purposes, as Part of this Constitution, when ratified by the Legislatures of three fourths of the several Sates, or by Conventions in three fourths thereof, as the one and the other Mode of Ratification may be proposed by the Congress; Provided that no Amendment which may be made prior to the Year One thousand eight hundred and eight shall in any Manner affect the first and fourth Clauses in the Ninth Section of the first Article; and that no State, without its Consent, shall be deprived of its equal Suffrage in the Senate.

Article. VI.

All Debts contracted and Engagements entered into, before the Adoption of this Constitution, shall be as valid against the United States under this Constitution, as under the Confederation.

This Constitution, and the Laws of the United States which shall be made in Pursuance thereof; and all Treaties made, or which shall be made, under the Authority of the United States, shall be the supreme Law of the Land; and the Judges in every State shall be bound thereby, any Thing in the Constitution or Laws of any State to the Contrary notwithstanding.

The Senators and Representatives before mentioned, and the Members of the several State Legislators, and all executive and judicial Officers, both of the United States and of the several States, shall be bound by Oath or Affirmation, to support this Constitution; but no religious Test shall ever be required as a Qualification to any Office or public Trust under the United States.

Article. VII.

The Ratification of the Conventions of nine States, shall be sufficient for the Establishment of this Constitution between the States so ratifying the Same.

The word, "the," being interlined between the seventh and eighth Lines of the first Page, the Word "Thirty" being partly written on an Erazure in the fifteenth Line of the first Page. The Words "is tried" being interlined between the thirty second and thirty third Lines of the first Page and the Word "the" being interlined between the forty third and forty fourth Lines of the second Page.

Attest William Jackson Secretary

Done in Convention by the Unanimous Consent of the States present the Seventeenth Day of September in the year of our Lord one thousand seven hundred and eighty seven and of the Independence of the United States of America the Twelfth In witness whereof We have hereunto subscribed our Names.

The Bill of Rights & Amendments

The conventions of a number of the states having, at the time of adopting the Constitution, expressed a desire, in order to prevent misconstruction or abuse of its power, that further declaratory and restrictive clauses should be added, and as extending the ground of public confidence in the government will best insure the beneficent ends of its institution; Resolved, by the Senate and House of Representatives of the United States of America, in congress assembled, two-thirds of both houses concurring, that the following articles be proposed to the legislatures of the several states, as amendments to the Constitution of the United States; all or any of which articles, when ratified by three-fourths of the said legislatures, to be valid to all intents and purposes as part of the said Constitution, namely:

Amendment 1 – Freedom of Religion, Press
Congress shall make no law respecting an establishment of religion or prohibiting the free exercise thereof; or abridging the freedom of speech, or of the press; or the right of the people peaceably to assemble, and to petition the government for a redress of grievances.

Amendment 2 – Right to Bear Arms
A well regulated militia, being necessary to the security of a free state, the right of the people to keep and bear arms, shall not be infringed.

Amendment 3 – Quartering of Soldiers
No soldier shall, in time of peace, be quartered in any house, without the consent of the owner, or in time of war, but in a manner to be prescribed by law.

Amendment 4 – Search and Seizure
The right of the people to be secure in their persons, houses, papers, and effects, against unreasonable searches and seizures, shall not be violated, and no warrants shall issue, but upon probable cause, supported by oath or affirmation, and particularly describing the place to be searched, and the persons or things to be seized.

Mike Gravel

Amendment 5 – Trial and Punishment, Compensation for Takings

No person shall be held to answer for a capital, or otherwise infamous crime, unless on a presentment or indictment of a grand jury, except in cases arising in the land or naval forces, or in the militia, when in actual service in time of war or public danger; nor shall any person be subject for the same offense to be twice put in jeopardy of life or limb; nor shall be compelled in any criminal case to be a witness against himself, not be deprived of life, liberty, or property, without due process of law; nor shall private property be taken for public use, without just compensation.

Amendment 6 – Right to Speedy Trial, Confrontation of Witnesses

In all criminal prosecution, the accused shall enjoy the right to a speedy and public trial, by an impartial jury of the state and district wherein the crime shall have been committed, which district shall have been previous ascertained by law, and to be informed of the nature and cause of the accusation; to be confronted with the witnesses against him; to have compulsory process for obtaining witnesses in his favor, and to have the assistance of counsel for his defense.

Amendment 7 – Trial by Jury in Civil Cases

In suits at common law, where the value in controversy shall exceed twenty dollars, the right of trial by jury shall be preserved, and no fact tried by a jury, shall be otherwise reexamined in any court of the United States, than according to the rules of common law.

Amendment 8 – Cruel and Unusual Punishment

Excessive bail shall not be required, nor excessive fines imposed, nor cruel and unusual punishments inflicted.

Amendment 9 – Construction of Constitution

The enumeration in the Constitution, of certain rights, shall not be construed to deny or disparage others retained by the people.

Amendment 10 – Powers of the States and People

The powers not delegated to the United States by the Constitution, nor prohibited by it to the states, are reserved to the states respectively, or to the people.

Amendment 11 – Judicial Limits

The Judicial power of the United States shall not be construed to extend to any suit in law or equity, commenced or prosecuted against one of the United States by Citizens of another State, or by Citizens or Subjects of any Foreign State.

Amendment 12 – Choosing the President, Vice-President

The Electors shall meet in their respective states, and vote by ballot for President and Vice-President, one of whom, at least, shall not be an inhabitant of the same state with themselves; they shall name in their ballots the person voted for as President, and in distinct ballots the person voted for as Vice-President, and they shall make distinct lists of all persons voted for as President, and of all persons voted for as Vice-President and of the number of votes for each, which lists they shall sign and certify, and transmit sealed to the seat of the government of the United States, directed to the President of the Senate;

The President of the Senate shall, in the presence of the Senate and House of Representatives, open all the certificates and the votes shall then be counted.

The person having the highest Number of votes for President, shall be the President, if such number be a majority of the whole number of Electors appointed; and if no person have such majority, then from the persons having the highest numbers not exceeding three on the list of those voted for as President, the House of Representatives shall choose immediately, by ballot, the President. But in choosing the President, the votes shall be taken by states, the representation from each state having one vote; a quorum for this purpose shall consist of a member or members from two-thirds of the states, and a majority of all the states shall be necessary to a choice. And if the House of Representatives shall not choose a President whenever the right of choice shall devolve upon them, before the fourth day of March next following, then the Vice-President shall act as President, as in the case of the death or other constitutional disability of the President.

The person having the greatest number of votes as Vice-President, if such number be a majority of the whole number of Electors appointed, and if no person have a majority, then from the two highest numbers on the list, the Senate shall choose the Vice-President; a quorum for the purpose shall consist of two-thirds of the whole number of Senators, and a majority of the whole number shall be necessary to a choice. But no person constitutionally ineligible to the office of President shall be eligible to that of Vice-President of the United States.

Amendment 13 – Slavery Abolished

Neither slavery nor involuntary servitude, except as a punishment for crime whereof the party shall have been duly convicted, shall exit within the United States, or any place subject to their jurisdiction. Congress shall have power to enforce this article by appropriate legislation.

Amendment 14 – Citizenship Rights

All persons born or naturalized in the United States, and subject to the jurisdiction thereof, are citizens of the United States and of the State wherein they reside. No State shall make or enforce any law which shall abridge the privileges or immunities of citizens of the United States; nor shall any State deprive any person of life, liberty, or property, without due process of law; nor deny to any person within its jurisdiction the equal protection of the laws.

Representatives shall be apportioned among the several States according to their respective numbers, counting the whole number of persons in each State, excluding Indians not taxed. But when the right to vote at any election for the choice of electors for President and Vice-President of the United States, Representatives in Congress, the Executive and Judicial officers of a State, or the member of the Legislature thereof, it denied to any of the male inhabitants of such State, being twenty-one years of age, and citizens of the United States, or in any way abridged, except for participation in rebellion or other crime, the basis of representation therein shall be reduced in the proportion which the number of such male citizens shall bear to the whole number of male citizens twenty-one years of age in such State.

No person shall be a Senator or Representative in Congress, or elector of President and Vice-President, or hold any office, civil or military, under the United States, or under any State, who, having previously taken an oath, as a member of Congress, or as an officer of the United States, or as a member of any State legislature, or as an executive or judicial officer of any State, to support the Constitution of the United States, shall have engaged in insurrection or rebellion against the same, or given aid or comfort to the enemies thereof. But Congress may by a vote of two-thirds of each House, remove such disability.

The validity of the public debt of the United States, authorized by law, including debts incurred for payment of pensions and bounties for services in suppressing insurrection or rebellion, shall not be questioned. But neither the United States nor any State shall assume or pay any debt or obligation incurred in aid of insurrection or rebellion against the United States, or any claim for the loss or emancipation of any slave; but all such debts, obligations and claims shall be held illegal and void.

The Congress shall have power to enforce, by appropriate legislation, the provisions of this article.

Amendment 15 – Race No Bar to Vote

The right of citizens of the United States to vote shall not be denied or abridged by the United States or by any State on account of race, color, or previous condition of servitude.

The Congress shall have power to enforce this article by appropriate legislation.

Amendment 16 – Status of Income Tax Clarified

The Congress shall have power to lay and collect taxes on incomes, from whatever source derived, without apportionment among the several States, and without regard to any census or enumeration.

Amendment 17 – Senators Elected by Popular Vote
The Senate of the United States shall be composed of two Senators from each State, elected by the people thereof, for six years; and each Senator shall have one vote. The electors of each State shall have the qualifications requisite for electors of the most numerous branch of State legislatures.

When vacancies happen in the representation of any State in the Senate, the executive authority of such State shall issue writs of election to fill such vacancies: Provided, That the legislature of any State may empower the executive thereof to make temporary appointments until the people fill the vacancies by election as the legislature may direct.

This amendment shall not be so construed as to affect the election or term of any Senator chosen before it becomes valid as part of the Constitution.

Amendment 18 – Liquor Abolished [Repealed by Amendment 21]
After one year from the ratification of this article the manufacture, sale, or transportation of intoxicating liquors within, the importation thereof into, or the exportation thereof from the United States and all territory subject to the jurisdiction thereof for beverage purposes is hereby prohibited.

The Congress and several States shall have concurrent power to enforce this article by appropriate legislation.

This article shall be inoperative unless it shall have been ratified as an amendment to the Constitution by the legislatures of the several States, as provided in the Constitution, within seven years from the date of the submission hereof to the States by the Congress.

Amendment 19 – Women's Suffrage
The right of citizens of the United States to vote shall not be denied or abridged by the United States or by any State on account of sex.

Congress shall have power to enforce this article by appropriate legislation.

Amendment 20 – Presidential, Congressional Terms

The terms of the President and Vice President shall end at noon on the 20th day of January, and the terms of Senators and Representatives at noon on the 3rd day of January, of the years in which such terms would have ended if this article had not been ratified; and the terms of their successors shall then begin.

The Congress shall assemble at least once in every year, and such meeting shall begin at noon on the 3rd day of January, unless they shall by law appoint a different day.

If, at the time fixed for the beginning of the term of the President, the President elect shall have died, the Vice President elect shall become President. If a President shall not have been chosen before the time fixed for the beginning of his term, or if the President elect shall have failed to qualify, then the Vice President elect shall act as President until a President shall have qualified; and the Congress may by law provide for the case wherein neither a President elect nor a Vice President elect shall have qualified, declaring who shall then act as President, or the manner in which one who is to act shall be selected, and such person shall act accordingly until a President or Vice President shall have qualified.

The Congress may by law provide for the case of the death of any of the persons from whom the House of Representatives may choose a President whenever the right of choice shall have devolved upon them, and for the case of the death of any of the persons from whom the Senate may choose a Vice President whenever the right of choice shall have devolved upon them.

Sections 1 and 2 shall take effect on the 15th day of October following the ratification of this article.

This article shall be inoperative unless it shall have been ratified as an amendment to the Constitution by the legislatures of three-fourths of the several States within seven years from the date of its submission.

Amendment 21 – Amendment 18 Repealed

The eighteenth article of amendment to the Constitution of the United States is hereby repealed.

The transportation or importation into any State, Territory, or possession of the United States for delivery or use therein of intoxicating liquors, in violation of the laws thereof, is hereby prohibited.

The article shall be inoperative unless it shall have been ratified as an amendment to the Constitution by conventions in the several States, as provided in the Constitution, within seven years from the date of the submission hereof to the States by the Congress.

Amendment 22 – Presidential Term Limits

No person shall be elected to the office of the President more than twice, and no person who has held the office of President, or acted as President, for more than two years of a term to which some other person was elected President shall be elected to the office of President, when this Article was proposed by the Congress, and shall not prevent any person who may be holding the office of President, or acting as President, during the term within which this Article becomes operative from holding the office of President or acting as President during the remainder of such term.

This article shall be inoperative unless it shall have been ratified as an amendment to the Constitution by the legislatures of three-fourths of the several States within seven years from the date of its submission to the States by the Congress.

Amendment 23 – Presidential Vote for District of Columbia

The District constituting the seat of Government of the United States shall appoint in such manner as the Congress may direct: A number of electors of President and Vice President equal to the whole number of Senators and Representatives of Congress to which the District would be entitled if it were a State, but in no event more than the least populous State; they shall be in addition to those appointed by the States, but they shall be considered, for the purposes of the election of President and Vice President, to be electors appointed by a State; and they shall meet in the District and perform such duties as provided by the twelfth article of amendment.

The Congress shall have power to enforce this article by appropriate legislation.

Amendment 24 – Poll Tax Barred

The right of citizens of the United States to vote in any primary or other election for President or Vice President, for electors for President or Vice President, or for Senator or Representative in Congress, shall not be denied or abridged by the United States or any State by reason of failure to pay any poll tax or other tax.

The Congress shall have power to enforce this article by appropriate legislation.

Amendment 25 – Presidential Disability and Succession

In case of the removal of the President from office or of his death or resignation, the Vice President shall become President.

Whenever there is a vacancy in the office of the Vice President, the President shall nominate a Vice President who shall take office upon confirmation by a majority vote of both Houses of Congress.

Whenever the President transmits to the President pro tempore of the Senate and the Speaker of the House of Representatives his written declaration that he is unable to discharge the powers and duties of his office, and until he transmits to them a written declaration to the contrary, such powers and duties shall be discharged by the Vice President as Acting President.

Whenever the Vice President and a majority of either the principal officers of the executive departments or of such other body as Congress may by law provide, transmit to the President pro tempore of the Senate and the Speaker of the House of Representatives their written declaration that the President is unable to discharge the powers and duties of his office, the Vice President shall immediately assume the powers and duties of the office of Acting President.

Thereafter, when the President transmits to the President pro tempore of the Senate and the Speaker of the House of Representatives his written declaration that no inability exists, he shall resume the powers and duties of his office unless the Vice President and a majority of either the principal officers of the executive department or of such other body as Congress may by law provide, transmit within four days to the President pro tempore of the Senate and the Speaker of the House of Representatives their written declaration that the President is unable to discharge the powers and duties of his office. Thereupon Congress shall decide the issue, assembling within forty-eight hours for that purpose if not in session. If the Congress, within twenty-one days after Congress is required to assemble, determines by two thirds vote of both Houses that the President is unable to discharge the powers and duties of his office, the Vice President shall continue to discharge the same as Acting President; otherwise, the President shall resume the powers and duties of his office.

Amendment 26 – Voting Age Set to 18 Years

The right of citizens of the United States, who are eighteen years of age or older, to vote shall not be denied or abridged by the United States or by any State on account of age.

The Congress shall have power to enforce this article by appropriate legislation.

Amendment 27 – Limiting Congressional Pay Increases

No pay, varying the compensation for the services of the Senator and Representatives, shall take effect, until an election of Representatives shall have intervened.

Appendix E

Charter of the United Nations

Preamble

WE THE PEOPLES OF THE UNITED NATIONS DETERMINED

➤ to save succeeding generations from the scourge of war, which twice in our lifetime has brought untold sorrow to mankind, and

➤ to reaffirm faith in fundamental human rights, in the dignity and worth of the human person, in the equal rights of men and women and of nations large and small, and

➤ to establish conditions under which justice and respect for the obligations arising from treaties and other sources of international law can be maintained, and

➤ to promote social progress and better standards of life in larger freedom,

AND FOR THESE ENDS

➤ to practice tolerance and live together in peace with one another as good neighbours, and

➤ to unite our strength to maintain international peace and security, and

➤ to ensure, by the acceptance of principles and the institution of methods, that armed forces shall not be used, save in the common interest, and

➤ to employ international machinery for the promotion of the economic and social advancement of all peoples,

HAVE RESOLVED TO COMBINE OUR EFFORTS TO ACCOMPLISH THESE AIMS

Accordingly, our respective Governments, through representatives assembled in the city of San Francisco, who have exhibited their full powers found to be in good and due form, have agreed to the present Charter of the United Nations and do hereby establish an international organization to be known as the United Nations.

CHAPTER 1

PURPOSES AND PRINCIPLES

Article 1
The Purposes of the United Nations are:

1. To maintain international peace and security, and to that end: to take effective collective measures for the prevention and removal of threats to the peace, and for the suppression of acts of aggression or other breaches of the peace, and to bring about by peaceful means, and in conformity with the principles of justice and international law, adjustment or settlement of international disputes or situations which might lead to a breach of the peace;

2. To develop friendly relations among nations based on respect for the principle of equal rights and self-determination of peoples, and to take other appropriate measures to strengthen universal peace;

3. To achieve international co-operation in solving international problems of an economic, social, cultural, or humanitarian character, and in promoting and encouraging respect for human rights and for fundamental freedoms for all without distinction as to race, sex, language, or religion; and

4. To be a centre for harmonizing the actions of nations in the attainment of these common ends.

Article 2

The Organization and its Members, in pursuit of the Purposes stated in Article 1, shall act in accordance with the following Principles:

1. The Organization is based on the principle of the sovereign equality of all its Members.

2. All Members, in order to ensure to all of them the rights and benefits resulting from membership, shall fulfill in good faith the obligations assumed by them in accordance with the present Charter.

3. All Members shall settle their international disputes by peaceful means in such a manner that international peace and security, and justice, are not endangered.

4. All members shall refrain in their international relations from the threat or use of force against the territorial integrity or political independence of any state, or in any other manner inconsistent with the Purposes of the United Nations.

5. All Members shall give the United Nations every assistance in any action it takes in accordance with the present Charter, and shall refrain from giving assistance to any state against which the United Nations is taking preventive or enforcement action.

6. The Organization shall ensure that states which are not Members of the United Nations act in accordance with these Principles so far as may be necessary for the maintenance of international peace and security.

7. Nothing contained in the present Charter shall authorize the United Nations to intervene in matters which are essentially within the domestic jurisdiction of any state or shall require the Members to submit such matters to settlement under the present Charter; but this principle shall not prejudice the application of enforcement measures under Chapter VII.

CHAPTER II

MEMBERSHIP

Article 3
The original Members of the United Nations shall be the states which, having participated in the United Nations Conference on International Organization at San Francisco, or having previously signed the Declaration by United Nations of 1 January 1942, sign the present Charter and ratify it in accordance with Article 110.

Article 4
1. Membership in the United Nations is open to all other peace-loving states which accept the obligations contained in the present Charter and, in the judgment of the Organization, are able and willing to carry out these obligations.

2. The admission of any such state to membership in the United Nations will be effected by a decision of the General Assembly upon the recommendation of the Security Council.

Article 5
A Member of the United Nations against which preventive or enforcement action has been taken by the Security Council may be suspended from the exercise of the rights and privileges of membership

by the General Assembly upon the recommendation of the Security Council. The exercise of these rights and privileges may be restored by the Security Council.

Article 6

A Member of the United Nations which has persistently violated the Principles contained in the present Charter may be expelled from the Organization by the General Assembly upon the recommendation of the Security Council.

CHAPTER III

ORGANS

Article 7

1.   There are established as the principal organs of the United Nations:

- a General Assembly
- a Security Council
- an Economic and Social Council
- a Trusteeship Council
- an International Court of Justice, and
- a Secretariat.

2. Such subsidiary organs as may be found necessary may be established in accordance with the present Charter.

Article 8

The United Nations shall place no restrictions on the eligibility of men and women to participate in any capacity and under conditions of equality in its principal and subsidiary organs.

CHAPTER IV

THE GENERAL ASSEMBLY

COMPOSITION

Article 9

The General Assembly shall consist of all the Members of the United Nations.

Each Member shall have not more than five representatives in the General Assembly.

FUNCTIONS and POWERS

Article 10

The General Assembly may discuss any questions or any matters within the scope of the present Charter or relating to the powers and functions of any organs provided for in the present Charter, and, except as provided in Article 12, may make recommendations to the Members of the United Nations or to the Security Council or to both on any such questions or matters.

Article 11

1. The General Assembly may consider the general principles of co-operation in the maintenance of international peace and security, including the principles governing disarmament and the regulation of armaments, and may make recommendations with regard to such principles to the Members or to the Security Council or to both.

2. The General Assembly may discuss any questions relating to the maintenance of international peace and security brought before it by any Member of the United Nations, or by the Security Council, or by a state which is not a Member of the United Nations in accordance with Article 35, paragraph 2, and, except as provided in Article 12, may make recommendations with regard to any such questions to the state or states concerned or to the Security Council or to both. Any such question on

which action is necessary shall be referred to the Security Council by the General Assembly either before or after discussion.

3. The General Assembly may call the attention of the Security Council to situations which are likely to endanger international peace and security.

4. The powers of the General Assembly set forth in this Article shall not limit the general scope of Article 10.

Article 12

1. While the Security Council is exercising in respect of any dispute or situation the functions assigned to it in the present Charter, the General Assembly shall not make any recommendation with regard to that dispute or situation unless the Security Council so requests.

2. The Secretary-General, with the consent of the Security Council, shall notify the General Assembly at each session of any matters relative to the maintenance of international peace and security which are being dealt with by the Security Council and shall similarly notify the General Assembly, or the Members of the United Nations if the General Assembly is not in session, immediately the Security Council ceases to deal with such matters.

Article 13

1. The General Assembly shall initiate studies and make recommendations for the purpose of:

a. promoting international co-operation in the political field and encouraging the progressive development of international law and its codification;

b. promoting international co-operation in the economic, social, cultural, educational, and health fields, and assisting in the realization of human rights and fundamental freedoms for all without distinction as to race, sex, language, or religion.

2. The further responsibilities, functions, and powers of the General Assembly with respect to matters mentioned in paragraph 1(b) above are set forth in Chapters IX and X.

Article 14
Subject to the provisions of Article 12, the General Assembly may recommend measures for the peaceful adjustment of any situation, regardless of origin, which it deems likely to impair the general welfare or friendly relations among nations, including situations resulting from a violation of the provisions of the present Charter setting forth the Purposes and Principles of the United Nations.

Article 15
1. The General Assembly shall receive and consider annual and special report from the Security Council; these reports shall include an account of the measures that the Security Council has decided upon or taken to maintain international peace and security.

2. The General Assembly shall receive and consider reports from the other organs of the United Nations.

Article 16
The General Assembly shall perform such functions with respect to the international trusteeship system as are assigned to it under Chapters XII and XIII, including the approval of the trusteeship agreements for areas not designated as strategic.

Article 17
1. The General Assembly shall consider and approve the budget of the Organization.

2. The expenses of the Organization shall be borne by the Members as apportioned by the General Assembly.

3. The General Assembly shall consider and approve any financial and budgetary arrangements with specialized agencies referred to in Article

57 and shall examine the administrative budgets of such specialized agencies with a view to making recommendations to the agencies concerned.

VOTING

Article 18

1. Each member of the General Assembly shall have one vote.

2. Decisions of the General Assembly on important questions shall be made by a two-thirds majority of the members present and voting. These questions shall include: recommendations with respect to the maintenance of international peace and security, the election of the non-permanent members of the Security Council, the election of the members of the Economic and Social Council, the election of members of the Trusteeship Council in accordance with paragraph 1 (c) of Article 86, the admission of new Members to the United Nations, the suspension of the rights and privileges of membership, the expulsion of Members, questions relating to the operation of the trusteeship system and budgetary questions.

3. Decisions on other questions, including the determination of additional categories of questions to be decided by a two-thirds majority, shall be made by a majority of the members present and voting.

Article 19

A Member of the United Nations which is in arrears in the payment of its financial contributions to the Organization shall have no vote in the General Assembly if the amount of its arrears equals or exceeds the amount of the contributions due from it for the preceding two full years. The General Assembly may, nevertheless, permit such a Member to vote if it is satisfied that the failure to pay is due to conditions beyond the control of the Member.

PROCEDURE

Article 20
The General Assembly shall meet in regular annual sessions and in such special sessions as occasion may require. Special sessions shall be convoked by the Secretary-General at the request of the Security Council or of a majority of the Members of the United Nations.

Article 21
The General Assembly shall adopt its own rules of procedure. It shall elect its President for each session.

Article 22
The General Assembly may establish such subsidiary organs as it deems necessary for the performance of its functions.

CHAPTER V

THE SECURITY COUNCIL

COMPOSITION

Article 23
1. The Security Council shall consist of fifteen Members of the United Nations. The Republic of China, France, the Union of Soviet Socialist Republics, the United Kingdom of Great Britain and Northern Ireland, and the United States of America shall be permanent members of the Security Council. The General Assembly shall elect ten other Members of the United Nations to be non-permanent members of the Security Council, due regard being specially paid, in the first instance to the contribution of Members of the United Nations to the maintenance of international peace and security and to the other purposes of the Organization, and also to equitable geographical distribution.

2. The non-permanent members of the Security Council shall be elected for a term of two years. In the first election of the non-permanent members after the increase of the membership of the Security Council

from eleven to fifteen, two of the four additional members shall be chosen for a term of one year. A retiring member shall not be eligible for immediate re-election.

3. Each member of the Security Council shall have one representative.

FUNCTIONS AND POWERS

Article 24

1. In order to ensure prompt and effective action by the United Nations, its Members confer on the Security Council primary responsibility for the maintenance of international peace and security, and agree that in carrying out its duties under this responsibility the Security Council acts on their behalf.

2. In discharging these duties the Security Council shall act in accordance with the Purposes and Principles of the United Nations. The specific powers granted to the Security Council for the discharge of these duties are laid down in Chapters VI, VII, VIII, and XII.

3. The Security Council shall submit annual and, when necessary, special reports to the General Assembly for its consideration.

Article 25

The Members of the United Nations agree to accept and carry out the decisions of the Security Council in accordance with the present Charter.

Article 26

In order to promote the establishment and maintenance of international peace and security with the least diversion for armaments of the world's human and economic resources, the Security Council shall be responsible for formulating, with the assistance of the Military Staff Committee referred to in Article 47, plans to be submitted to the Members of the United Nations for the establishment of a system for the regulation of armaments.

VOTING

Article 27

1. Each member of the Security Council shall have one vote.

2. Decisions of the Security Council on procedural matters shall be made by an affirmative vote of nine members.

3. Decision of the Security Council on all other matters shall be made by an affirmative vote of nine members including the concurring votes of the permanent members; provided that, in decisions under Chapter VI, and under paragraph 3 of Article 52, a party to a dispute shall abstain from voting.

PROCEDURE

Article 28

1. The Security Council shall be so organized as to be able to function continuously. Each member of the Security Council shall for this purpose be represented at all times at the seat of the Organization.

2. The Security Council shall hold periodic meetings at which each of its members may, if it so desires, be represented by a member of the government or by some other specially designated representative.

3. The Security Council may hold meetings at such places other than the seat of the Organization as in its judgment will best facilitate its work.

Article 29

The Security Council may establish such subsidiary organs as it deems necessary for the performance of its functions.

Article 30

The Security Council shall adopt its own rules of procedure, including the method of selecting its President.

Article 31

Any Member of the United Nations which is not a member of the Security Council may participate, without vote, in the discussion of any question brought before the Security Council whenever the latter considers that the interests of that Member are specially affected.

Article 32

Any Member of the United Nations which is not a member of the Security Council or any state which is not a Member of the United Nations, if it is a party to a dispute under consideration by the Security council, shall be invited to participate, without vote, in the discussion relating to the dispute. The Security Council shall lay down such conditions as it deems just for the participation of a state which is not a Member of the United Nations.

CHAPTER VI

PACIFIC SETTLEMENT OF DISPUTES

Article 33

1. The parties to any dispute, the continuance of which is likely to endanger the maintenance of international peace and security, shall, first of all, seek a solution by negotiation, enquiry, mediation, conciliation, arbitration, judicial settlement, resort to regional agencies or arrangements, or other peaceful means of their own choice.

2. The Security Council shall, when it deems necessary, call upon the parties to settle their dispute by such means.

Article 34

The Security Council may investigate any dispute, or any situation which might lead to international friction or give rise to a dispute, in order to determine whether the continuance of the dispute or situation is likely to endanger the maintenance of international peace and security.

Article 35

1. Any Member of the United Nations may bring any dispute, or any situation of the nature referred to in Article 34, to the attention of the Security Council or of the General Assembly.

2. A state which is not a Member of the United Nations may bring to the attention of the Security Council or of the General Assembly any dispute to which it is a party if it accepts in advance, for the purposes of the dispute, the obligations of pacific settlement provided in the present Charter.

3. The proceedings of the General Assembly in respect of matters brought to its attention under this Article will be subject to the provisions of Articles 11 and 12.

Article 36

1. The Security Council may, at any stage of a dispute of the nature referred to in Article 33 or of a situation of like nature, recommend appropriate procedures or methods of adjustment.

2. The Security Council should take into consideration any procedures for the settlement of the dispute which have already been adopted by the parties.

3. In making recommendations under this Article the Security Council should also take into consideration that legal disputes should as a general rule be referred by the parties to the International Court of Justice in accordance with the provisions of the Statute of the Court.

Article 37

1. Should the parties to a dispute of the nature referred to in Article 33 fail to settle it by the means indicated in that Article, they shall refer it to the Security Council.

2. If the Security Council deems that the continuance of the dispute is in fact likely to endanger the maintenance of international peace and security, it shall decide whether to take action under Article 36 or to recommend such terms of settlement as it may consider appropriate.

Article 38

Without prejudice to the provisions of Articles 33 to 37, the Security Council may, if all the parties to any dispute so request, make recommendations to the parties with a view to a pacific settlement of the dispute.

CHAPTER VII

ACTION WITH RESPECT TO THREATS TO THE PEACE, BREACHES OF THE PEACE, AND ACTS OF AGGRESSION

Article 39

The Security Council shall determine the existence of any threat to the peace, breach of the peace, or act of aggression and shall make recommendations, or decide what measures shall be taken in accordance with Articles 41 and 42, to maintain or restore international peace and security.

Article 40

In order to prevent an aggravation of the situation, the Security Council may, before making the recommendations or deciding upon the measures provided for in Article 39, call upon the parties concerned to comply with such provisional measures as it deems necessary or desirable. Such provisional measures shall be without prejudice to the rights, claims, or position of the parties concerned. The Security Council shall duly take account of failure to comply with such provisional measures.

Article 41

The Security Council may decide what measures not involving the use of armed force are to be employed to give effect to its decisions, and it may call upon the Members of the United Nations to apply such measures. These may include complete or partial interruption of economic relations and of rail, sea, air, postal, telegraphic, radio, and other means of communication, and the severance of diplomatic relations.

Article 42

Should the Security Council consider that measures provided for in Article 41 would be inadequate or have proved to be inadequate, it may take such action by air, sea, or land forces as may be necessary to maintain or restore international peace and security. Such action may include demonstrations, blockade, and other operations by air, sea, or land forces of Members of the United Nations.

Article 43

1. All Members of the United Nations, in order to contribute to the maintenance of international peace and security, undertake to make available to the Security Council, on its call and in accordance with a special agreement or agreements, armed forces, assistance, and facilities, including rights of passage, necessary for the purpose of maintaining international peace and security.

2. Such agreement or agreements shall govern the numbers and types of forces, their degree of readiness and general location, and the nature of the facilities and assistance to be provided.

3. The agreement or agreements shall be negotiated as soon as possible on the initiative of the Security Council. They shall be concluded between the Security Council and Members or between the Security Council and groups of Members and shall be subject to ratification by the signatory states in accordance with their respective constitutional processes.

Article 44

When the Security Council has decided to use force it shall, before calling upon a Member not represented on it to provide armed forces in fulfillment of the obligations assumed under Article 43, invite that Member, if the Member so desires, to participate in the decisions of the Security Council concerning the employment of contingents of that Member's armed forces.

Article 45

In order to enable the United Nations to take urgent military measures, Members shall hold immediately available national air-force contingents for combined international enforcement action. The strength and degree of readiness of these contingents and plans for their combined action shall be determined within the limits laid down in the special agreement or agreements referred to in Article 43, by the Security Council with the assistance of the Military Staff Committee.

Article 46

Plans for the application of armed forces shall be made by the Security Council with the assistance of the Military Staff Committee.

Article 47

1. There shall be established a Military Staff Committee to advise and assist the Security Council on all questions relating to the Security Council's military requirements for the maintenance of international peace and security, the employment and command of forces placed at its disposal, the regulation of armaments, and possible disarmament.

2. The Military Staff Committee shall consist of the Chiefs of Staff of the permanent members of the Security Council or their representatives. Any Member of the United Nations not permanently represented on the Committee shall be invited by the Committee to be associated with it when the efficient discharge of the Committee's responsibilities requires the participation of that Member in its work.

3. The Military Staff Committee shall be responsible under the Security Council for the strategic direction of any armed forces placed at the disposal of the Security Council. Questions relating to the command of such forces shall be worked out subsequently.

4. The Military Staff Committee, with the authorization of the Security Council and after consultation with appropriate regional agencies, may establish regional sub-committees.

Article 48

1. The action required to carry out the decisions of the Security Council for the maintenance of international peace and security shall be taken by all the Members of the United Nations or by some of them, as the Security Council may determine.

2. Such decisions shall be carried out by the Members of the United Nations directly and through their action in the appropriate international agencies of which they are members.

Article 49

The Members of the United Nations shall join in affording mutual assistance in carrying out the measures decided upon by the Security Council.

Article 50

If preventive or enforcement measures against any state are taken by the Security Council, any other state, whether a Member of the United Nations or not, which finds itself confronted with special economic problems arising from the carrying out of those measures shall have to right to consult the Security Council with regard to a solution of those problems.

Article 51

Nothing in the present Charter shall impair the inherent right of individual or collective self-defence if an armed attack occurs against a Member of the United Nations, until the Security Council has taken measures necessary to maintain international peace and security. Measures taken by Members in the exercise of this right of self-defence shall be immediately reported to the Security Council and shall not in any way affect the authority and responsibilities of the Security Council under the present Charter to take at any time such action as it deems necessary in order to maintain or restore international peace and security.

CHAPTER VIII

REGIONAL ARRANGEMENTS

Article 52

1. Nothing in the present Charter precludes the existence of regional arrangements or agencies for dealing with such matters relating to the maintenance of international peace and security as are appropriate for regional action provided that such arrangements or agencies and their activities are consistent with the Purposes and Principles of the United Nations.

2. The Members of the United Nations entering into such arrangements or constituting such agencies shall make every effort to achieve pacific settlement of local disputes through such regional arrangements or by such regional agencies before referring them to the Security Council.

3. The Security Council shall encourage the development of pacific settlement of local disputes through such regional arrangements or by such regional agencies either on the initiative of the states concerned or by reference from the Security Council.

4. This Article in no way impairs the application of Articles 34 and 35.

Article 53

1. The Security Council shall, where appropriate, utilize such regional arrangements or agencies for enforcement action under its authority. But no enforcement action shall be taken under regional arrangements or by regional agencies without the authorization of the Security council, with the exception of measures against any enemy state, as defined in paragraph 2 of this Article, provided for pursuant to Article 107 or in regional arrangements directed against renewal of aggressive policy on the part of any such states, until such time as the Organization may, on request of the Governments concerned, be charged with the responsibility for preventing further aggression by such a state.

2. The term enemy state as used in paragraph 1 of this Article applies to any state which during the Second World War has been an enemy of any signatory of the present Charter.

Article 54

The Security Council shall at all times be kept fully informed of activities undertaken or in contemplation under regional arrangements or by regional agencies for the maintenance of international peace and security.

CHAPTER IX

INTERNATIONAL ECONOMIC AND SOCIAL CO-OPERATION

Article 55

With a view to the creation of conditions of stability and well-being which are necessary for peaceful and friendly relations among nations based on respect for the principle of equal rights and self-determination of peoples, the United Nations shall promote:

a. Higher standards of living, full employment, and conditions of economic and social progress and development;

b. Solutions of international economic, social, health, and related problems; and international cultural and educational cooperation; and

c. Universal respect for, and observance of, human rights and fundamental freedoms for all without distinction as to race, sex, language, or religion.

Article 56

All Members pledge themselves to take joint and separate action in co-operation with the Organization for the achievement of the purposes set forth in Article 55.

Article 57

1. The various specialized agencies, established by intergovernmental agreement and having wide international responsibilities, as defined in their basic instruments, in economic, social, cultural, educational, health, and related fields, shall be brought into relationship with the United Nations in accordance with the provisions of Article 63.

2. Such agencies thus brought into relationship with the United Nations are hereinafter referred to as specialized agencies.

Article 58

The Organization shall make recommendations for the co-ordination of the policies and activities of the specialized agencies.

Article 59

The Organization shall, where appropriate, initiate negotiations among the states concerned for the creation of any new specialized agencies required for the accomplishment of the purposes set forth in Article 55.

Article 60

Responsibility for the discharge of the functions of the Organization set forth in this Chapter shall be vested in the General Assembly and, under the authority of the General Assembly, in the Economic and Social Council, which shall have for this purpose the powers set forth in Chapter X.

CHAPTER X

THE ECONOMIC AND SOCIAL COUNCIL

COMPOSITION

Article 61

1. The Economic and Social Council shall consist of fifty-four Members of the United Nations elected by the General Assembly.

2. Subject to the provisions of paragraph 3, eighteen members of the Economic and Social Council shall be elected each year for a term of three years. A retiring member shall be eligible for immediate re-election.

3. At the first election after the increase in the membership of the Economic and Social Council from twenty-seven to fifty-four members, in addition to the members elected in place of the nine members whose term of office expires at the end of that year, twenty-seven additional members shall be elected. Of these twenty-seven additional members, the term of office of nine members so elected shall expire at the end of one year, and of nine other members at the end of two years, in accordance with arrangements made by the General Assembly.

4. Each member of the Economic and Social Council shall have one representative.

FUNCTIONS AND POWERS

Article 62
1. The Economic and Social Council may make or initiate studies and reports with respect to international economic, social, cultural, educational, health, and related matters and may make recommendations with respect to any such matters to the General Assembly to the Members of the United Nations, and to the specialized agencies concerned.

2. It may make recommendations for the purpose of promoting respect for, and observance of, human rights and fundamental freedoms for all.

3. It may prepare draft conventions for submission to the General Assembly, with respect to matters falling within its competence.

4. It may call, in accordance with the rules prescribed by the United Nations, international conferences on matters falling within its competence.

Article 63

1. The Economic and Social Council may enter into agreements with any of the agencies referred to in Article 57, defining the terms on which the agency concerned shall be brought into relationship with the United Nations. Such agreements shall be subject to approval by the General Assembly.

2. It may co-ordinate the activities of the specialized agencies through consultation with and recommendations to such agencies and through recommendations to the General Assembly and to the Members of the United Nations.

Article 64

1. The Economic and Social Council may take appropriate steps to obtain regular reports from the specialized agencies. It may make arrangements with the Members of the United Nations and with the specialized agencies to obtain reports on the steps taken to give effect to its own recommendations and to recommendations on matters falling within its competence made by the General Assembly.

2. It may communicate its observations on these reports to the General Assembly.

Article 65

The Economic and Social Council may furnish information to the Security Council and shall assist the Security Council upon its request.

Article 66

1. The Economic and Social Council shall perform such functions as fall within its competence in connexion with the carrying out of the recommendations of the General Assembly.

2. It may, with the approval of the General Assembly, perform services at the request of Members of the United Nations and at the request of specialized agencies.

3. It shall perform such other functions as are specified elsewhere in the present Charter or as may be assigned to it by the General Assembly.

VOTING

Article 67
Each member of the Economic and Social Council shall have one vote.

Decisions of the Economic and Social Council shall be made by a majority of the members present and voting.

PROCEDURE

Article 68
The Economic and Social Council shall set up commissions in economic and social fields and for the promotion of human rights, and such other commissions as may be required for the performance of its functions.

Article 69
The Economic and Social Council shall invite any Member of the United Nations to participate, without vote, in its deliberations on any matter of particular concern to that Member.

Article 70
The Economic and Social Council may make arrangements for representatives of the specialized agencies to participate, without vote, in its deliberations and in those of the commissions established by it, and for its representatives to participate in the deliberations of the specialized agencies.

Article 71
The Economic and Social Council may make suitable arrangements for consultation with non-governmental organizations which are concerned with matters within its competence. Such arrangements may be made with international organizations and, where appropriate, with national organizations after consultation with the Member of the United Nations concerned.

Article 72

1. The Economic and Social Council shall adopt its own rules of procedures, including the method of selecting its President

2. The Economic and Social Council shall meet as required in accordance with its rules, which shall include provision for the convening of meetings on the request of a majority of its members.

CHAPTER XI

DECLARATION REGARDING NON-SELF-GOVERNING TERRITORIES

Article 73

Member of the United Nations which have or assume responsibilities for the administration of territories whose peoples have not yet attained a full measure of self-government recognize the principle that the interests of the inhabitants of these territories are paramount, and accept as a sacred trust the obligation to promote to the utmost, within the system of international peace and security established by the present Charter, the well-being of the inhabitants of these territories, and, to this end:

a. to ensure, with due respect for the culture of the peoples concerned, their political, economic, social, and educational advancement, their just treatment, and their protection against abuses;

b. to develop self-government, to take due account of the political aspirations of the peoples, and to assist them in the progressive development of their free political institutions, according to the particular circumstances of each territory and its peoples and their varying stages of advancement;

c. to further international peace and security;

d. to promote constructive measures of development, to encourage research, and to co-operate with one another and, when and where appropriate, with specialized international bodies with a view to the practical achievement of the social, economic, and scientific purposes set forth in this Article; and

e. to transmit regularly to the Secretary-General for information purposes, subject to such limitation as security and constitutional considerations may require, statistical and other information of a technical nature relating to economic, social, and educational conditions in the territories for which they are respectively responsible other than those territories to which Chapters XII and XIII apply.

Article 74

Members of the United Nations also agree that their policy in respect of the territories to which this Chapter applies, no less than in respect of their metropolitan areas, must be based on the general principle of good-neighbourliness, due account being taken of the interests and well-being of the rest of the world, in social, economic, and commercial matters.

CHAPTER XII

INTERNATIONAL TRUSTEESHIP SYSTEM

Article 75

The United Nations shall establish under its authority an international trusteeship system for the administration and supervision of such territories as may be placed thereunder by subsequent individual agreements. These territories are hereinafter referred to as trust territories.

Article 76

1. The basic objectives of the trusteeship system, in accordance with the Purposes of the United Nations laid down in Article 1 of the present Charter, shall be:

2. To further international peace and security;

3. To promote the political, economic, social, and educational advancement of the inhabitants of the trust territories, and their progressive development towards self-government or independence as may be appropriate to the particular circumstances of each territory and its peoples and the freely expressed wishes of the peoples concerned, and as may be provided by the terms of each trusteeship agreement;

4. To encourage respect for human rights and for fundamental freedoms for all without distinction as to race, sex, language, or religion, and to encourage recognition of the interdependence of the peoples of the world; and

5. To ensure equal treatment in social, economic, and commercial matters for all Members of the United Nations and their nationals, and also equal treatment for the latter in the administration of justice, without prejudice to the attainment of the foregoing objectives and subject to the provisions of Article 80.

Article 77

1. The trusteeship system shall apply to such territories in the following categories as may be placed thereunder by means of trusteeship agreements:

   a. territories now held under mandate;
   b. territories which may be detached from enemy states as a result of the Second World War; and
   c. territories voluntarily placed under the system by states responsible for their administration.

2. It will be a matter for subsequent agreement as to which territories in the foregoing categories will be brought under the trusteeship system and upon what terms.

Article 78

The trusteeship system shall not apply to territories which have become Members of the United Nations, relationship among which shall be based on respect for the principle of sovereign equality.

Article 79

The terms of trusteeship for each territory to be placed under the trusteeship system, including any alteration or amendment, shall be agreed upon by the states directly concerned, including the mandatory power in the case of territories held under mandate by a Member of the United Nations, and shall be approved as provided for in Articles 83 and 85.

Article 80

1. Except as may be agreed upon in individual trusteeship agreements, made under Articles 77, 79, and 81, placing each territory under the trusteeship system, or until such agreements have been concluded, nothing in this Chapter shall be construed in or of itself to alter in any manner the rights whatsoever of any states or any peoples or the terms of existing international instruments to which Members of the United Nations may respectively be parties.

2. Paragraph 1 of this Article shall not be interpreted as giving grounds for delay or postponement of the negotiation and conclusion of agreements for placing mandated and other territories under the trusteeship system as provided for in Article 77.

Article 81

The trusteeship agreement shall in each case include the terms under which the trust territory will be administered and designate the authority which will exercise the administration of the trust territory. Such authority, hereinafter called the administering authority, may be one or more states or the Organization itself.

Article 82

There may be designated, in any trusteeship agreement, a strategic area or areas which may include part or all of the trust territory to which the agreement applies, without prejudice to any special agreement or agreements made under Article 43.

Article 83

1. All functions of the United Nations relating to strategic areas, including the approval of the terms of the trusteeship agreements and of their alteration or amendment shall be exercised by the Security Council.

2. The basic objectives set forth in Article 76 shall be applicable to the people of each strategic area.

3. The Security Council shall, subject to the provisions of the trusteeship agreements and without prejudice to security considerations, avail itself of the assistance of the Trusteeship Council to perform those functions of the United Nations under the trusteeship system relating to political, economic, social, and educational matters in the strategic areas.

Article 84

It shall be the duty of the administering authority to ensure that the trust territory shall play its part in the maintenance of international peace and security. To this end the administering authority may make use of volunteer forces, facilities, and assistance from the trust territory in carrying out the obligations towards the Security Council undertaken in this regard by the administering authority, as well as for local defence and the maintenance of law and order within the trust territory.

Article 85

1. The functions of the United Nations with regard to trusteeship agreements for all areas not designated as strategic, including the approval of the terms of the trusteeship agreements and of their alteration or amendment, shall be exercised by the General Assembly.

2. The Trusteeship Council, operating under the authority of the General Assembly shall assist the General Assembly in carrying out these functions.

CHAPTER XIII

THE TRUSTEESHIP COUNCIL

COMPOSITION

Article 86

The Trusteeship Council shall consist of the following Members of the United Nations:

a. those Members administering trust territories;
b. such of those Members mentioned by name in Article 23 as are not administering trust territories; and
c. as many other Members elected for three-year terms by the General Assembly as may be necessary to ensure that the total number of members of the Trusteeship Council is equally divided between those Members of the United Nations which administer trust territories and those which do not.

Each member of the Trusteeship Council shall designate one specially qualified person to represent it therein.

FUNCTIONS AND POWERS

Article 87

The General Assembly and, under its authority, the Trustee Council, in carrying out their functions, may:

a. consider reports submitted by the administering authority;
b. accept petitions and examine them in consultation with the administering authority;
c. provide for periodic visits to the respective trust territories at times agreed upon with administering authority; and
d. take these and other actions in conformity with the terms of the trusteeship agreements.

Article 88

The Trusteeship Council shall formulate a questionnaire on the political, economic, social, and educational advancement of the inhabitants of each trust territory, and the administering authority for each trust territory within the competence of the General Assembly shall make an annual report to the General Assembly upon the basis of such questionnaire.

VOTING

Article 89

1. Each member of the Trusteeship Council shall have one vote.

2. Decisions of the Trusteeship Council shall be made by a majority of the members present and voting.

PROCEDURE

Article 90

1. The Trusteeship Council shall adopt its own rules of procedure, including the method of selecting its President.

2. The Trusteeship Council shall meet as required in accordance with its rules, which shall include provision for the convening of meetings on the request of a majority of its members.

Article 91

The Trusteeship Council shall, when appropriate, avail itself of the assistance of the Economic and Social Council and of the specialized agencies in regard to matters with which they are respectively concerned.

CHAPTER XIV

THE INTERNATIONAL COURT OF JUSTICE

Article 92

The International Court of Justice shall be the principal judicial organ of the United Nations. It shall function in accordance with the annexed Statute, which is based upon the Statute of the Permanent Court of International Justice and forms an integral part of the present Charter.

Article 93

1. All Members of the United Nations are *ipso facto* parties to the Statute of the International Court of Justice.

2. A state which is not a Member of the United Nations may become a party to the Statute of the International Court of Justice on conditions to be determined in each case by the General Assembly upon the recommendation of the Security Council.

Article 94

1. Each Member of the United Nations undertakes to comply with the decision of the International Court of Justice in any case to which it is a party.

2. If any party to a case fails to perform the obligations incumbent upon it under a judgment rendered by the Court, the other party may have recourse to the Security Council, which may, if it deems necessary, make recommendations or decide upon measures to be taken to give effect to the judgment.

Article 95

Nothing in the present Charter shall prevent Members of the United Nations from entrusting the solution of their differences to other tribunals by virtue of agreements already in existence or which may be concluded in the future.

Article 96

1. The General Assembly or the Security Council may request the International Court of Justice to give an advisory opinion on any legal question.

2. Other organs of the United Nations and specialized agencies, which may at any time be so authorized by the General Assembly, may also request advisory opinions of the Court on legal questions arising within the scope of their activities.

CHAPTER XV

THE SECRETARIAT

Article 97

The Secretariat shall comprise a Secretary-General and such staff as the Organization may require. The Secretary-General shall be appointed by the General Assembly upon the recommendation of the Security Council. He shall be the chief administrative officer of the Organization.

Article 98

The Secretary-General shall act in that capacity in all meetings of the General Assembly, of the Security Council, of the Economic and Social Council, and of the Trusteeship Council, and shall perform such other functions as are entrusted to him by these organs. The Secretary-General shall make an annual report to the General Assembly on the work of the Organization.

Article 99

The Secretary-General may bring to the attention of the Security Council any matter which in his opinion may threaten the maintenance of international peace and security.

Article 100

1. In the performance of their duties the Secretary-General and the staff shall not seek or receive instructions from any government or from any other authority external to the Organization. They shall refrain from

any action which might reflect on their position as international officials responsible only to the Organization.

2. Each member of the United Nations undertakes to respect the exclusively international character of the responsibilities of the Secretary-General and the staff and not to seek to influence them in the discharge of their responsibilities.

Article 101

1. The staff shall be appointed by the Secretary-General under regulations established by the General Assembly.

2. Appropriate staffs shall be permanently assigned to the Economic and Social Council, the Trusteeship Council, and, as required, to other organs of the United Nations. These staffs shall form a part of the Secretariat.

3. The paramount consideration in the employment of the staff and in the determination of the conditions of service shall be the necessity of securing the highest standards of efficiency, competence, and integrity. Due regard shall be paid to the importance of recruiting the staff on as wide a geographical basis as possible.

CHAPTER XVI

MISCELLANEOUS PROVISIONS

Article 102

1. Every treaty and every international agreement entered into by any Member of the United Nations after the present Charter comes into force shall as soon as possible be registered with the Secretariat and published by it.

2. No party to any such treaty or international agreement which has not been registered in accordance with the provisions of paragraph 1 of this Article may invoke that treaty or agreement before any organ of the United Nations.

Article 103

In the event of a conflict between the obligations of the Members of the United Nations under the present Charter and their obligations under any other international agreement, their obligations under the present Charter shall prevail.

Article 104

The Organization shall enjoy in the territory of each of its Members such legal capacity as may be necessary for the exercise of its functions and the fulfillment of its purposes.

Article 105

1. The Organization shall enjoy in the territory of each of its Members such privileges and immunities as are necessary for the fulfillment of its purposes.

2. Representatives of the Members of the United Nations and officials of the Organization shall similarly enjoy such privileges and immunities as are necessary for the independent exercise of their functions in connexion with the Organization.

3. The General Assembly may make recommendations with a view to determining the details of the application of paragraphs 1 and 2 of this Article or may propose conventions to the Members of the United Nations for this purpose.

CHAPTER XVII

TRANSITIONAL SECURITY ARRANGEMENTS

Article 106

Pending the coming into force of such special agreements referred to in Article 43 as in the opinion of the Security Council enable it to begin the exercise of its responsibilities under Article 42, the parties to the Four-Nation Declaration, signed at Moscow, 30 October 1943, and France, shall, in accordance with the provisions of paragraph 5 of that

Declaration, consult with one another and as occasion requires with other Members of the United Nations with a view to such joint action on behalf of the Organization as may be necessary for the purpose of maintaining international peace and security.

Article 107
Nothing in the present Charter shall invalidate or preclude action, in relation to any state which during the Second World War has been an enemy of any signatory to the present Charter, taken or authorized as a result of that war by the Governments having responsibility for such action.

CHAPTER XVIII

AMENDMENTS

Article 108
Amendments to the present Charter shall come into force for all members of the United Nations when they have been adopted by a vote of two thirds of the members of the General Assembly and ratified in accordance with their respective constitutional processes by two thirds of the Members of the United Nations, including all the permanent members of the Security Council.

Article 109
1. A General Conference of the Members of the United Nations for the purpose of reviewing the present Charter may be held at a date and place to be fixed by a two-thirds vote of the members of the General Assembly and by a vote of any nine members of the Security Council. Each Member of the United Nations shall have one vote in the conference.

2. Any alteration of the present Charter recommended by a two-thirds vote of the conference shall take effect when ratified in accordance with their respective constitutional processes by two thirds of the Members of the United Nations including all the permanent members of the Security Council.

3. If such a conference has not been held before the tenth annual session of the General Assembly following the coming into force of the present Charter, the proposal to call such a conference shall be placed on the agenda of that session of the General Assembly, and the conference shall be held if so decided by a majority vote of the members of the General Assembly and by a vote of any seven members of the Security Council.

CHAPTER XIX

RATIFICATION AND SIGNATURE

Article 110

1. The present Charter shall be ratified by the signatory states in accordance with their respective constitutional processes.

2. The ratifications shall be deposited with the Government of the United States of America, which shall notify all the signatory states of each deposit as well as the Secretary-General of the Organization when he has been appointed.

3. The present Charter shall come into force upon the deposit of ratifications by the Republic of China, France, the Union of Soviet Socialist Republics, the United Kingdom of Great Britain and Northern Ireland, and the United States of America, and by a majority of the other signatory states. A protocol of the ratifications deposited shall thereupon be drawn up by the Government of the United States of America which shall communicate copies thereof to all the signatory states.

4. The states signatory to the present Charter which ratify it after it has come into force will become original Members of the United Nations on the date of the deposit of their respective ratifications.

Article 111

The present Charter, of which the Chinese, French, Russian, English, and Spanish texts are equally authentic, shall remain deposited in the archives of the Government of the United States of America. Duly certified copies thereof shall be transmitted by that Government to the Governments of the other signatory states.

IN FAITH WHEREOF the representatives of the Governments of the United Nations have signed the present Charter.

DONE at the city of San Francisco the twenty-sixth day of June, one thousand nine hundred and forty-five.

Appendix F

Notable Quotations

People can decide with as much propriety on the...amendment [of the Constitution]...as ourselves, for I do not conceive that we...have more wisdom or possess more virtue than those who will come after us. —*George Washington, 1787*

The people were, in fact, the fountain of all power, and by resorting to them, all difficulties were got over. They could alter constitutions as they pleased. —*James Madison, 1787*

All power is originally in the People and should be exercised by them in person, if that could be done with convenience, or even little difficulty. —*James Wilson*

Unless the mass retains sufficient control over...government, [representatives] will be perverted...to the perpetuation of wealth and power in the individuals and their families selected for the trust. —*Thomas Jefferson, 1812*

The basis of our political system is the right of the people to make and to alter their constitutions of government. —*George Washington*

Each generation has a right to choose for itself the form of government it believes is promotive of its happiness. —*Thomas Jefferson*

In those words [the Preamble of the Constitution] it is agreed, and with every passing moment it is re-agreed, that the people of the United

States shall be self governed. To that fundamental enactment, all other provisions of the Constitution, all statutes, all administrative decrees, are subsidiary and dependent. All other purposes, whether individual or social, can find their legitimate scope and meaning only as they conform to the one basic purpose—that the citizens of this nation shall make and shall obey their own laws, shall be at once their own subjects and masters. —*Alexander Meiklejohn, 1960*

The genius of the Constitution rests not in any static meaning it may have had in a world that is dead and gone, but in the adaptability of its great principles to cope with current problems and with present needs. —*Justice J. Brennan, Jr., 1985*

Index

O

Organization for Economic Co-operation and Development 51, 131
Overbye, Thomas 57

P

Pentagon Papers ix, xvi, 91, 92, 101, 119
Pfaff, William 126
Philadelphia II 14, 16, 143, 145, 152, 154–157, 160
Prohibition 63, 65, 74

R

Reeve, Emory xvi
Republican Party 32
Rifkin, Jeremy 60
Rockefeller, Governor Nelson 74
Roosevelt, President Franklin D. 123

S

Senate Finance Committee 32
Sentencing Project 74
Shafer Commission 70
Slavery 72, 136–140, 186
Social Security 9, 10, 37, 38
Space-based solar power 59, 61, 116
Speech or Debate Clause of the Constitution 102
States' rights 140
Switzerland 12, 131, 138

T

Tocqueville, Alexis de 12

CPSIA information can be obtained
at www.ICGtesting.com
Printed in the USA
FSHW021352250719
60387FS

9 781434 343154